CLASSIC ROCK
NUMBER 03

MUELLER STATE PARK and ELEVENMILE CANYON

COLORADO

by
Bob D'Antonio

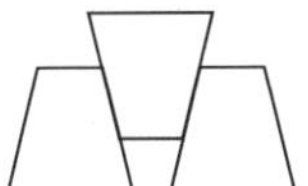

Chockstone Press
Evergreen, Colorado
1996

Classic Rock Climbs: Mueller State Park and Elevenmile Canyon, Colorado

Cover Photo: *Bits and Pieces* (5.11+ ★★★) on The Fortress, Elevenmile Canyon. Photo by Bob D'Antonio. Unless noted otherwise, all photographs are by the author.

ISBN: 1-57540-025-1 *Classic Rock Climbs* series
1-57540-031-6 *Mueller State Park and Elevenmile Canyon, Colorado*

Published and distributed by:
Chockstone Press, Inc.
Post Office Box 3505
Evergreen, CO 80437-3505

DEDICATION

This book is dedicated to my Mother, Judy D'Antonio. Her love, support and sense of adventure have been with me through all my endeavors.

ACKNOWLEDGMENTS

A book of this scope would not be possible without the help of many people. First, I'd like to thank my best friend and wife of 21 years, Laurel. Without her support and understanding of my love for climbing, none of my climbing dreams would have come true.

Most of these areas hold a special place in my climbing heart, I lived in the Colorado Springs area for seven years and have many fond memories of climbing in the Garden, Elevenmile Canyon, Pike's Peak and Mueller State Park. Thanks to Richard Aschert, Lew Hoffman, Bob Robertson, Larry Kledzik, Chuck Carlson, Stewart Green and all the other partners I had the pleasure to climb with.

Thanks to all the climbers who gave me information, comments and proofread parts of the manuscript, including Stewart Green, Mark Milligan, Mark Van Horn, Dave Dangle, Mark Rolofson, Steve Cheyney, Kerry Gunter, Richard Aschert, Bob Robertson, Peter Gallagher and Glen Schuler. A big special thanks to my friend Jon Hardy for the use of his Powerbook and to Mark Sonnenfeld for all his help and advice that made this project a lot easier. Thank you to Betty Alf for help with the road maps. Special thanks go to Stewart Green for all his help in proofreading the material for this book, the use of his excellent photos and access to his vast store of knowledge of the area.

TABLE OF CONTENTS

Ian Spencer-Green on *Skid Marks* (5.11c), River Wall, Elevenmle Canyon, Colorado. Photo: Stewart M. Green

INTRODUCTION

MUELLER STATE PARK and ELEVENMILE CANYON

The mountain region west of Pikes Peak, the snowy 14,110-foot-high sentinel of the southern Front Range, is a largely nondescript area of low, rolling mountains creased with broad valleys and sharp canyons. A piney forest coats the hillsides above the grass-choked valleys. A closer look at the area reveals a host of off-the-beaten track natural wonders, including Florissant Fossil Beds National Monument, as well as a couple of Colorado's finest rock climbing areas on the crags of Elevenmile Canyon and on lofty domes above Four Mile Creek.

The South Platte River, rising on the snowy north flank of Mt. Lincoln and the Continental Divide at Hoosier Pass, slowly unwinds like a giant serpent across broad South Park. In the far southwestern corner of the park, the river pools in immense Elevenmile Reservoir before plunging into an abrupt canyon sliced through the pink granite of the Pikes Peak batholith. Here the swift river, using its snowmelt-laden waters as an abrasive cutting tool, has incised a narrow, steep-walled gorge lined with soaring cliffs and slabs, broken by grassy side-canyons, flanked by rounded mountains, and blanketed with ponderosa pine forest.

Elevenmile Canyon, easily accessed via an improved dirt road from Lake George to the dam at the canyon's head, is a rock climber's delight. Here is every type of rock route imaginable— fierce Yosemite-style cracks, delicate slabs, and chickenhead-studded faces. Long multi-pitch affairs scale some of the longer slabs and walls, but most of the lines are short and sweet. It's a place that has found a home for both traditional routes as well as modern sport climbs. The cracks and longer routes here, offering marvelous protection possibilities, are done in a traditional style. The bald faces, however, yield little natural pro and are consequently bolted. It's this calm meeting of divergent climbing styles and ethics that makes Elevenmile so attractive. The place had been ignored by climbers for so long that the great 1980s ethical debates passed Elevenmile right by. Still climbers need to comport themselves properly—this is, after all, public land and it's a privilege to recreate on it. A few ugly incidents have reared their heads in the last few years. Some routes have chipped holds and some have had unnecessary bolts added.

The canyon is one of the very best beginner and moderate climbing areas in Colorado. Excellent learning lines abound on the crags. Some of the best include *The Staircase* and *Zendance* on Arch Rock; *Happy Trails* on Elevenmile Dome; *Sunshine Slab*, *Schooldaze*, and *Guide's Route* on Turret Dome; and *Armaj Das* on Pine Cone Dome. Honed crack-masters will enjoy jamming *Peisker Crack* on Sports Crag, *Breakfast in America*, and *Teale*

THE AUTHOR ON *RAINY DAY WOMANIZER* (5.11c R), DOME ROCK. PHOTO: STEWART M. GREEN.

Tower Route. Top sport climbers can find the upper end at The Spray Wall, including the excellent *Only Entertainment* and *Pagan Wisdom*.

The Four Mile Dome Area, lying east of Elevenmile Canyon and Florissant Fossil Beds National Monument, spreads along Four Mile Creek in the morning shade of Pikes Peak. The climbing cliffs are within the Dome Rock wildlife area in Mueller State Park, a large enclave of semi-wild mountain country managed by the Colorado Division of State Parks.

The Four Mile Dome area is beautiful country. Tall, angular crags and huge slabs seamed with cracks jut above Four Mile Creek as it meanders through dense willow thickets and wind-rippled grass on the broad valley floor. Dark forests of spruce, fir, and pine, broken by glades of quaking aspen and wildflower-strewn meadows, blanket the rocky hillsides. The Four Mile region is an outstanding natural area that forms a rich and diverse habitat for numerous wildlife species including eagles, deer, elk, bear, bobcat, wild turkey, and, most importantly, bighorn sheep. Bighorns, Colorado's majestic state animal, have long used this hidden valley as a crucial wintering and lambing area and remains one of the best lower-elevation bighorn ranges in the state. Climbers and hikers need to be aware that this land is set aside for the wildlife. Recreation is a mere by-product. Use it wisely or risk losing its climbing possibilities. Posted signs, found on the trails, inform users of bighorn area closures.

The climbing along Four Mile Creek is absolutely stunning. Towering, Tuolume Meadows-type domes loom above the pastoral valley. Dome Rock dominates the valley with its 800-foot-high granite bulk looming atop the eastern rim. The other domes, including blocky Four Mile Dome and the clean sweep of West Rock, lift their grey shoulders high above wooded ridges and shallow side-canyons. Classic routes abound here. Soaring crack lines offer hard jamming tests. Remember to tape your hands. Some of the coarse granite is studded with fine, sharp crystals that can shred the hands. The slab climbing here, however, is heavenly. The Four Mile slabs are literally some of Colorado's finest friction opportunities. These routes, most of them multi-pitch lines, edge up delicate faces protected by old bolts placed on the lead by bold activists.

Elevenmile Canyon and Four Mile Dome area are both spectacular arenas to pursue the climbing passion. Neither has seen lots of activity like more popular havens outside Denver, Boulder, and Colorado Springs. Come and sample the best these granite areas have to offer, but remember to climb softly and leave no trace of your passage besides a touch of chalk on the rock.

—Stewart M. Green

IAN SPENCER-GREEN ON *PAGAN WISDOM* (5.11C), SPRAY WALL. PHOTO BY STEWART M. GREEN

CLIMBING DANGERS AND SAFETY Once you put on your climbing shoes or rope up, you run the chance of getting hurt or killed. Some of the routes in this guide are dangerous and should only be attempted by climbers confident in his or her ability to climb at a high level of skill. Don't be fooled by numbers, a 5.9 on a sport route is much easier than a 5.9 at 12,000 ft. on Pike's Peak. If you have done most of your climbing in a gym you should limit your climbing to sport routes. Do not attempt to climb traditional routes without knowing how to place gear and set natural belays.

I have tried to give the most accurate information that I could find to get you to the climbs. Once you are there it is your responsibility to take care of your partner and yourself. If a climb looks too hard, don't do it. If a climb looks too scary, don't do it. Ratings are very subjective and should be taken with a grain of salt. A 5.10 with four bolts in 20 feet is much different from a 5.10 with natural gear every 15 feet. If you are just learning how to climb, hook up with a competent guide, you will learn more in one day than you would in weeks on your own.

Self preservation should always come first. If you are feeling weak, go climb something easy. If you are going to solo a route, do it alone and away from people, they don't want to see your body mangled at the bottom of some cliff. Use common sense. Good judgment can save your life, bad judgment can kill you. This is a guidebook and nothing more. It can't help you climb better, it won't get you up a climb, and it won't minimize the dangers of climbing real rock in the real world.

ETHICS Most of the climbs in this book were established in the 1970s and '80s. Most of these climbs are traditional climbs, they were done from the ground up with natural gear and bolts that were placed for protection on lead from the ground up. Please respect the accomplishments of the first ascent party. Don't add bolts to established routes, if a bolt needs to be replaced ask the first ascent party's permission. If you want to change the character of a route in any way, ask the first ascent party. Too many people in the Colorado Springs area have taken it upon themselves to change routes without asking. Don't be one of them. If you are trying to do a route and it is too hard, don't alter the route, just work at getting better. A sport route with hard moves and a lot of bolts is just that, hard. A traditional climb with hard moves and difficult gear placements should be left as a testimony to a climber's ability to climb difficult rock in less than ideal conditions.

Chipping and altering routes, especially established routes, not only degrades the first ascent effort, it degrades climbing itself. Most climbers don't care if you hang, grab or fall a hundred times on a route. Climbers do care if you change the route by altering the rock or protection. If the overhanging side of the Spray Wall at Elevenmile Canyon is the future of climbing, with all its chip holds, then personally I think we have none.

In the end, how you ascend a climb is more important than reaching the top. Take pride in how you climb. If you're not up to doing a route in its natural state, don't change the character of a route just to make it easier. Take your frustrations to the rock gym, that's what it is there for. If you find a blank piece of rock, don't chip, look a little harder and you'll find rock with holds on it. What we do today affects what will happens tomorrow. Take pride in how you climb, we are leaving a legacy for other climbers who will come after us. Learn about your sport and read about the history of the areas you are climbing in. Not only will you get a historical perspective, it will enhance your climbing visit. Join the Access Fund and get involved in access issues. Most of all, realize that the rock is not infinite. There is only so much to go around, respect the rock and the privilege that we have of climbing on it.

RATING SYSTEM This guide uses the Yosemite Decimal System, the system that most climbers are familiar with. The routes in this book range in difficulty from 5.0 to 5.13. A 5.10 slab route could be easier or harder than a 5.10 crack. Use this system with a grain of salt, some routes at the same grade can be completely different. An R or an X after the grade of a route denotes added danger and one should be competent at or above the level of the climb. An R or X rated climb means that there is little or no protection, and a fall could mean serious injury or death. Remember that all climbs could be R or X rated climbs.

Some routes will have a (+) or (–). This is a subgrade and only means that the route is either easier (–) or harder (+) than a "straight" rating. Just to confuse you a little more, the sub grades of a, b, c, d, are used to rate climbs 5.10 or harder. A 5.10a is usually a lot easier than a 5.10d. Most routes are rated by the most difficult move. A climb with a single move of 5.11 may feel easier than a climb with many moves of 5.10.

A Roman numeral from I to III might follow the technical grade, this indicates the commitment and time factor involved in climbing the route. A Grade I takes a strong party one to two hours to climb, where as a Grade III would or should take a strong party four to five hours to climb. This does not take into account the time walking to and from a climb. An R or a X following the grade means that this route is *serious* and should only be attempted by someone competent at a level above the grade listed.

A free climbing rack for the routes in this book should include RPs, a set of wired Stoppers, Aliens, TCUs, a set of Friends or other camming devices, eight or so Quickdraws, four runners of various lengths, a few free carabiners, a 165-foot rope and an extra rope for rappels. Having all the gear in the world won't help you if you don't know how to use it. Take the time to gain confidence in your ability to place natural protection.

After all is said and done, it is up to you to respect the rocks and our sport. It is also up to you to bring the proper gear to a climb and scope out the climb before you do it. It is your responsibility to respect the public and private lands that we are permitted to climb on. You should look at climbing as privilege, not just a right. Too many areas have been closed down due to irresponsible climbers, don't be one of the those whose selfish acts hurt the rest of the climbing community.

ledge
right-facing corner or dihedral
left-facing corner or dihedral
crack width
bolt or piton
line of climb
arête
roof or overhang
fixed belay station
serious fall potential
death fall potential
wide crack or chimney

ACCOMMODATIONS Colorado Springs is Colorado's second largest city and offers all the benefits of a large city. Campgrounds are limited and family oriented. There are a number of campgrounds located on National Forest lands.There is a also the Colorado Springs Youth Hostel, located at 17 North Farragut Avenue that offers warm and comfortable beds at reasonable rates. Restaurants run from Taco Bells to five-star eateries. Good cheap food can be found at a number of restaurants. My favorite places to eat are: La Casita, 1331 S. Nevada; Old Chicago, downtown Colorado Springs; The Manitou Bakery in downtown Manitou Springs; and Poor Richard's Espresso Bar on Boulder and Tejon in downtown Colorado Springs.

WEATHER Spring, summer and fall are the climbing seasons for the area, usually extending from May to September. The best conditions and stable weather are from March to October. Precipitation, mostly afternoon showers, is likely in June and July.

EMERGENCY SERVICES In case of emergency contact Colorado Springs Police at 911. Hospitals in Colorado Springs are: Penrose Hospital, 2215 North Cascade, 630-3300 or St. Francis, East Pikes Peak, 473-6830.

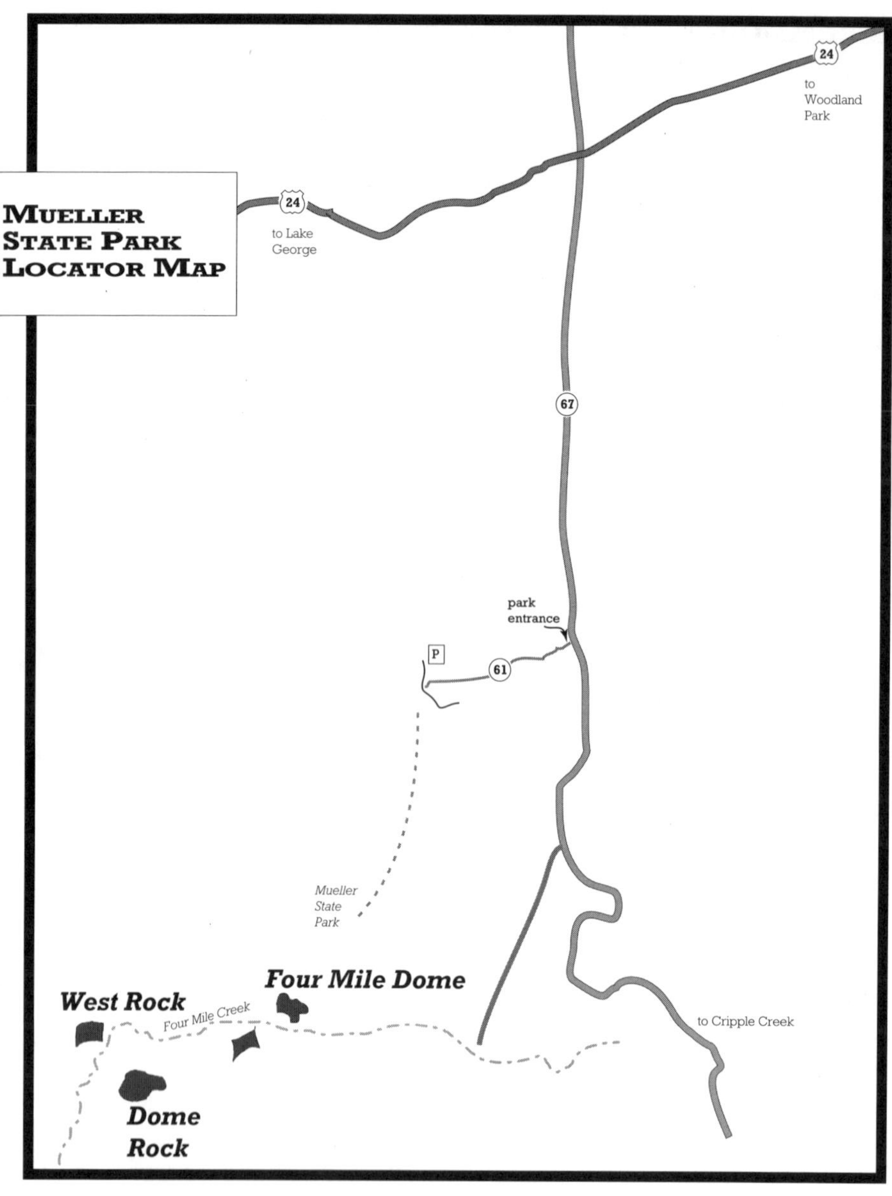
Mueller State Park Locator Map
24
to Lake George
24
to Woodland Park
67
park entrance
P
61
Mueller State Park
Four Mile Dome
West Rock
Four Mile Creek
Dome Rock
to Cripple Creek

SECTION ONE

MUELLER STATE PARK

Mueller State Park is a little known climbing area located northwest of Pikes Peak. Four Mile Creek wanders its way through this beautiful valley full of granite domes, wildflowers and wildlife. The area offers some of the best slab climbing in all of Colorado. The park has a number of large domes ranging in heights from 200 to 700 feet. The park is also home to one of the largest Bighorn Sheep herds in the state. This is a remote area and sees very few climbers. Be considerate when climbing here, the rangers do not have any problems with the climbers, but that could change with the acts of a few negligent climbers. This is also a state Wildlife Refuge, so be aware of your impact on Bighorns when they are in their prime lambing time (December to April). The area also offers great mountain biking, hiking, wildlife viewing, trail running, and cross country skiing.

CLIMBING HISTORY Being a fairly new climbing area, the history of the park is short and brief and can be summed up in two words: Richard Aschert! Well almost, Richard was the driving force in the mid-eighties when a majority of the routes where put up. Earl Wiggins was one of the first climbers to explore and climb on Four Mile Dome, with his brother Art, he put up *Blood, Sweat and Tears* which was later free climbed by Leonard Coyne and Mark Rolofson. Coyne and Rolofson returned the next year (1978) and added a another good route, *Voyeur's Odyssey* (5.11–), on the large west face.

The 1980s saw a renewed interest in the area with a number of excellent and difficult routes completed on West Rock, Dome Rock and Four Mile Dome. Most of these routes were the work of Bob Robertson, Dave Dangle, Kerry Gunter, Eric Harp, Harvey Miller and Richard Aschert, who was the main driving force.

HOW TO GET THERE From Colorado Springs take U.S. 24 west to the town of Divide. Turn left on highway 67 follow this for 3.5 miles to the park entrance. Follow the trail for four miles along Four Mile Creek to the Domes. Four Mile Dome (the largest) will be the first dome on your left.

West Rock lies farther west. Both climbing areas are on the south side of the creek. Dome Rock sits on the north side of the creek and is directly across the valley from Four Mile Dome.

FOUR MILE DOME

With routes up to eight pitches long, south and west-facing exposure, this dome has some of the longest slab routes in the South Platte area.

1 **Yellow Thang (11b) P1:** Start in a short, left-facing corner. Follow crac ks up to a belay ledge (165 ft.). **P2:** Follow an easy ramp up face, past two bolts to a belay. **P3:** Follow aline of bolts, past a seam to a belay at the base of a large ramp. **P4:** Go up ramp for 150 feet to belay. P5: Follow prominent exit crack to the top. FA: Richard Aschert, Chris Hill, 1987.

2 **Blood, Sweat and Tears (10–) ★ P1:** Go up crack past two pin s and abolt to a large ledge. **P2:** Follow a left-facing corner, to a ledge. Traverse left, past a bolt to 5.9 handcrack. Follow handcrack to belay. **P3:** Follow crack up overhang to left-facing corner to a large ledge. **P4:** Follow cracks to top. Gear: Full rack to #3 Friend. FA: Art and Earl Wiggins, 1976. FFA: Leonard Coyne and Mark Rolofson, 1978.

3 **Voyeur's Odyssey (11–) ★★ P1:** Scramble up the ramp to large ldege. Look for bolts out on the face. Climb past bolts (crux) to large ledge, traverse right to belay. **P2:** Up face past two bolts, traverse right to a nice fingercrack. **P3:** Climb face, past two bolts, to a crack. Go up the crack to large belay ledge. **P4:** Traverse left, to left-facing corner. Follow corner to the top. Gear: Full rack to #4 Friend. FA: Leonard Coyne and Mark Rolofson, 1978.

4 **Bold Runner (11c R) ★★** Up ramp to middle of the southwest face. **P1:** Up short inconspicuous handcrack to belay ledge. **P2:** Goes up left-leaning seam to main waterstreak and belay. **P3:** Follow a line of bolts up the face to the summit. FA: Bob Robertson, Richard Aschert and Peter Gallagher, 1986.

5 **The Unforgiven (10+) P1:** Up the handcrack just left of a huge, left-facing corner. **P2:** Continue up cracks in corner to a right-leaning seam. Follow seam out right up to ledge. **P3:** Up water groove, past seven bolts to summit. FA: Kerry Gunter, 1990.

6 **Pale Rider (11c) P1:** Up dogleg crack in the center of the face, past two bolts (crux) to belay ledge. **P2:** Follow crack to belay ledge. **P3:** Follow crack out left, over a bulge to face to the summit. FA: Kerry Gunter, 1990.

7 **The White One (10) P1:** Up the obvious corner for two pitches to the top. FA: Richard Aschert and Chris Hill.

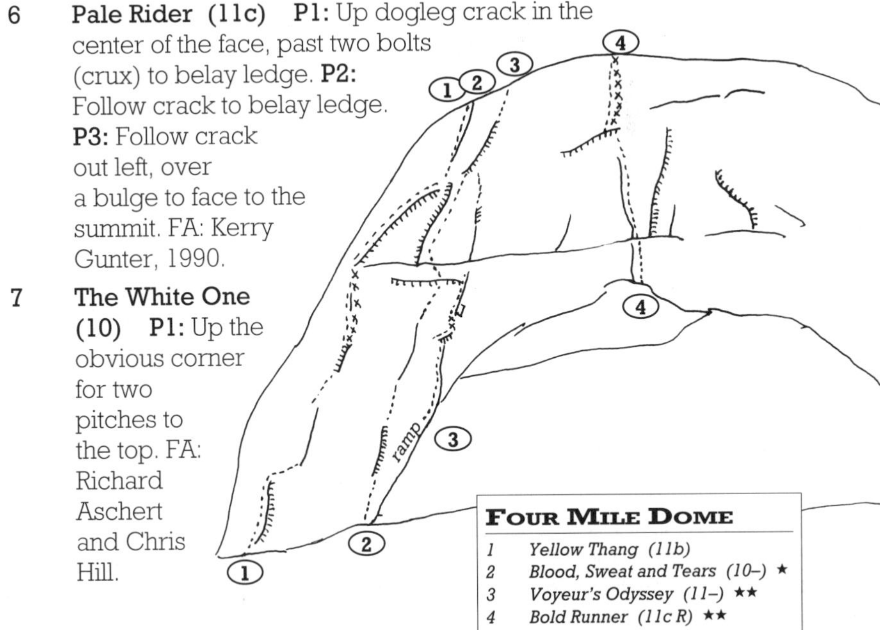

DOME ROCK

1 *Hands Away (10+)* ★★
2 *Rainy Day Womanizing (11+)* ★
3 *Dome Roof (11)* ★★
4 *For Vegetarians Only (8)* ★
5 *Ironing Board (11 R)* ★★

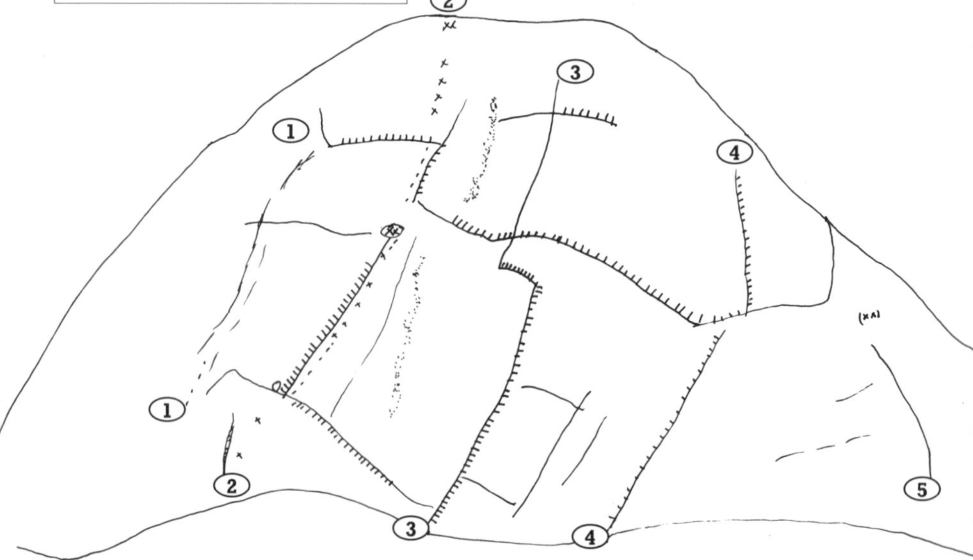

DOME ROCK

1 **Hands Away (10+) ★★** Pitch 1 traverses an obvious wide crack. Pitch 2 fires up the perfect handcrack. Gear: Friends to #4, doubles from #1.5 and up, Quickdraws. FA: Kerry Gunter and Lou Kalina, 1989.

2 **Rainy Day Womanizing (11+) ★** Pitch 1 goes up a low-angle slab past one bolt. Pitch 2 takes the obvious obtuse dihedral and fingercrack to face past five bolts, belay in the obvious alcove. Pitch 3 goes right on loose rock past three bolts to the top. Gear: Small camming gear, medium Friends, Stoppers and Quickdraws. FA: Mike Johnson and Lou Kalina, 1986.

3 **Dome Roof (11) ★★** Pitch 1 goes up a steep slab past bolts to a belay. Pitch 2 follow crack out a huge roof. FA: Richard Aschert, Fred Aschert and Bob Robertson, 1986.

4 **For Vegetarians Only (8) ★** This route follows the obvious dihedral system just left of *Ironing Board* for four pitches to the top. Gear: To #3.5 Friend. FA: Ed Pearsall and Richard Aschert, 1986.

5 **Ironing Board (11 R) ★★** Pitch 1 goes up a hard to protect thin crack/seam. Pitch 2 climbs straight up the face to the top. Gear: RPs, Stoppers and camming gear. FA: Richard Aschert and Ed Pearsall.

WEST ROCK

West-facing exposure and exceptional slab routes up to three-pitches long. This rock is well worth the four-mile walk.

Descent: The best descent is to go to the northeast and find a tree with rappel slings and do a 50-foot rappel to the ground. You can also do three rappels down the rock from the last pitch of She's a Dyke.

1 **Cling on Treachery (12–) ★★** This route starts on the far left side (north) of the rock. Pitch 1 climbs the face past seven bolts to a belay at a crack. Pitch 2 continues up slab to a belay below a roof. Pitch 3 goes left over the bulge/roof to the top of the rock. Gear: Medium Friends to #2.5, medium Stoppers and Quickdraws. FA: Richard Aschert and Eric Harp, 1986.

2 **She's a Dyke (10) ★★★** One of the best routes on the rock. Pitch 1 follows the major dike system on the left side of the rock. Pitches 2 and 3 continue up the dike to the top. Gear: Medium Friends and Quickdraws. FA: Bob Robertson and Harvey Miller, 1986.

3 **Lady Bug (11+/12– R) ★★** Excellent slab climbing with some long runouts on the last pitch. Pitch 1 goes up slab to a belay at the first pitch of *She's a Dyke*. Pitch 2 goes left up a steep slab past ten bolts. Pitch 3 (R) continues up slab past four bolts in 140 feet. Gear: Medium Friends, many Quickdraws. FA: Bob Robertson and Richard Aschert, 1985.

4 **Max Overhead (12–) ★★** This route tackles the impressive roof in the middle of the crag. Pitches 1 and 2 go up the slab to the second belay on *She's a Dyke*. Pitch 3 climbs out the roof past some pins to the summit headwall. Gear: Light medium rack and Quickdraws. FA: Richard Aschert and Dave Dangle, 1985.

5 **Kamikaze Clone (12) ★★★** Impressive climbing with a hard and continuous crux pitch. Pitch 1 climbs a short slab past four bolts to a ledge on the right side of the rock. Pitch 2 climbs the obvious right-facing dihedral to a belay stance with bolts. Pitch 3 goes straight up the steep headwall to the last belay on *She's a Dyke*. Gear: Medium rack with Friends up to #3 and Quickdraws. FA: Richard Aschert and Eric Harp, 1986.

6 **Escape from Clone (11–) ★** Pitches 1 and 2 are the same as *Kamikaze Clone*. Pitch 3 traverses right to the base of the obvious overhanging handcrack. Pitch 4 climbs the crack to the top of the rock. Gear: Friends to #3.5, Stoppers and Quickdraws. FA: Ed Pearsall and Dave Bower, 1986.

7 **Beyond the Eighth Dimension (12)** This one-pitch route starts on a ledge on the right side of the rock. Gear: Quickdraws. FA: Eric Harp, 1986.

8 **Mr. Chicago (12–) ★★** This route climbs the striking arête on a huge boulder right off the trail below West Rock. Gear: Quickdraws. FA: Bob D'Antonio and Chuck Carlson (aka Mr. Chicago), 1994.

WEST ROCK

1 *Cling on Treachery (12–) ★★*
2 *She's a Dyke (10) ★★★*
3 *Lady Bug (11+/12– R) ★★*
4 *Max Overhead (12–) ★★*
5 *Kamikaze Clone (12) ★★★*
6 *Escape from Clone (11–) ★*
7 *Beyond the Eighth Dimension (12)*

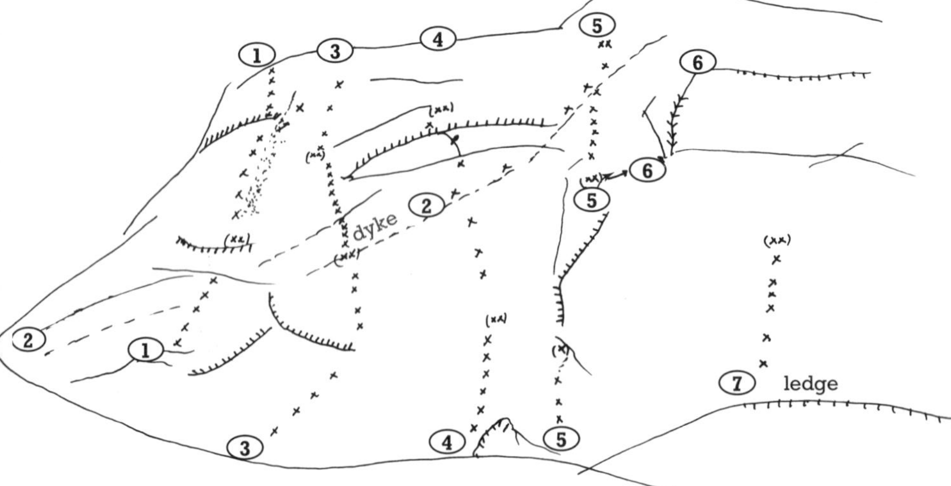

WEST ROCK
1 Cling on Treachery (12–) ★★
2 She's a Dyke (10) ★★★
4 Max Overhead (12–) ★★
5 Kamikaze Clone (12) ★★★
1
2
4
5

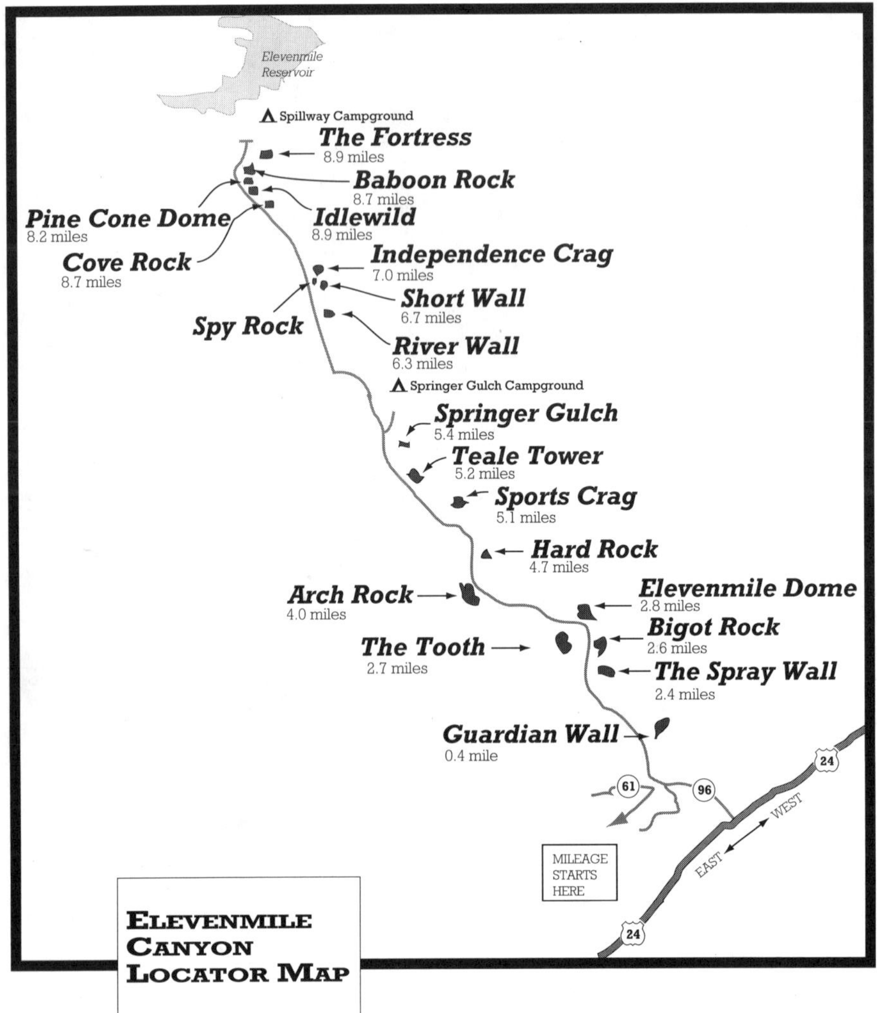

Elevenmile Canyon Locator Map

SECTION TWO

ELEVENMILE CANYON

The early climbing history of Elevenmile Canyon is vague at best. Technical climbing seems to have started in the early 1960s with members from the Colorado Mountain Club ascending a number of the easy routes as practice for greater climbs in other areas. Routes on Turret Dome, Pine Cone Dome and Arch Rock more than likely had first ascents done by memebers of the Colorado Mountain Club. Although these routes were far from the technical standard reach, in other areas they serve the purpose of the day.

The canyon's new route activity lay dormant for a number of years. Climbers ignored the canyon potential for new routes, most of their attention given instead the Garden of the Gods and areas in the nearby South Platte. Things seem to change in the mid-1970s, when Brian Teale and Dan Morrison, guides working for Turret Dome Climbing School, ascended many of the moderate classics. Though not overly difficult, these routes seem to open the eyes of other climbers to the potential the canyon possess for new routes. Peter Gallagher and Peter Williams first free ascent of the *Teale Tower* (5.11–) and Gallagher and John Kato's first ascent of *Fly or Fry* (5.11 R) in the late 1970s were major jumps in technical difficulty and laid the foundation for future development.

The early 1980s brought a new route feeding frenzy. As the number of routes increased, the standard of difficulty rose quickly, matching that at the other cliffs in the Pikes Peak areas. Climbs and climbers that stand out from this period were Chris Peisker's ascent of a thin overhanging crack of the Sports Crag. *The Peisker Crack* (5.12c) was a major achievement and brought a level of difficulty never seen before in the canyon. I and Mark Rolofson jumped on the new route bandwagon and added two new difficult routes in one day to the Sport Crag. *Moonage Daydreaming* (5.12) and *Shock the Monkey* (5.12–) were a team effort and started a new route rage seldom seen in the Pikes Peak area. It seemed as if every week a new 5.12 was done in the canyon. By the mid-'80s there were over 35 new 5.12s done on various cliffs in the canyon. I was at the forefront of development along with Richard Aschert, Dale Goddard, Mark Milligan, Mark Rolofson and Neil Cannon, adding a number of new routes to the ever-growing list of new hard routes. Numerous classic hard routes were put up in the mid-'80s: *Little Kingdom* (5.13), *The Intimidator* (5.12c), *The Vatican* (5.12), *Here's To Future Ways* (5.12c) and *The Sanctuary* (5.12c) are just a few of many great routes done in this period. As the 1980s were coming to a close, climbers in the Pikes Peak are discovered new areas like Shelf Road and San Luis Valley and the activity in Elevenmile slowed to a snail's pace.

The early 1990s brought some renewed interest in Elevenmile and a number of new hard routes were put up by a handful of local climbers. Glenn Schuler, Mark Milligan, Kevin McLaughlin and Bill Schmauser were the main movers during this time. Though the pace of development fell short of that of the Eighties, Elevenmile seems to have found its place among the excellent climbs areas around Colorado Springs. There are numerous crags within a 10- to 15-minute walk of the road, waiting for development. The future of new route development in Elevenmile Canyon does not lie in the chipping or gluing of holds nor the indiscriminate use of bolts. The future of Elevenmile Canyon is the many natural lines waiting to be ascended by the climbers willing to put the in proper time and effort.

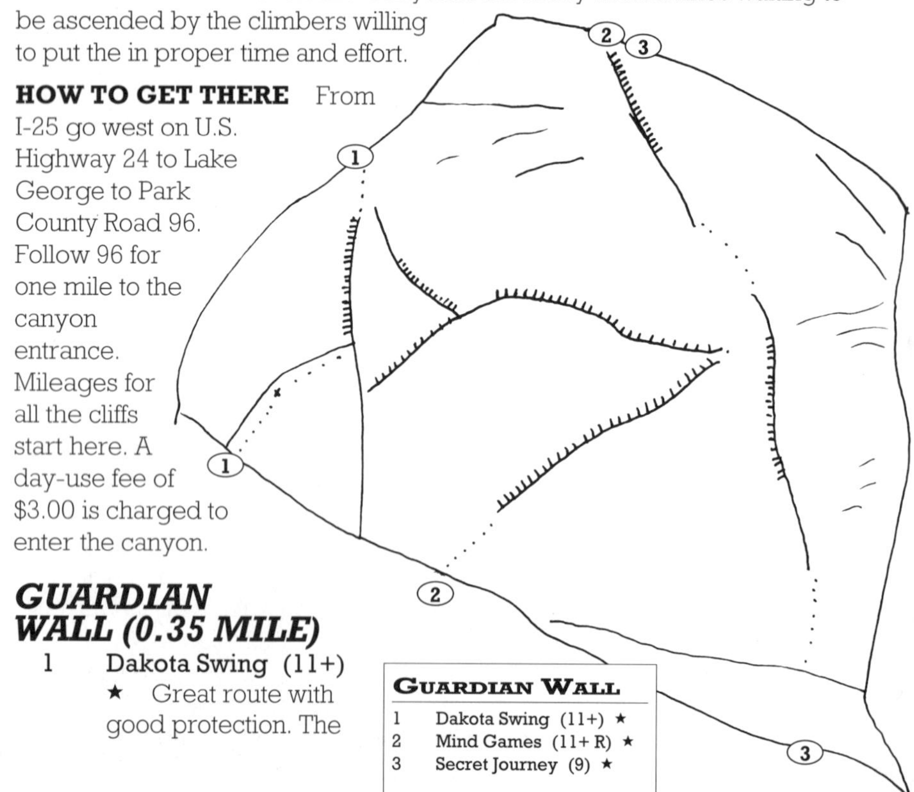

HOW TO GET THERE From I-25 go west on U.S. Highway 24 to Lake George to Park County Road 96. Follow 96 for one mile to the canyon entrance. Mileages for all the cliffs start here. A day-use fee of $3.00 is charged to enter the canyon.

GUARDIAN WALL (0.35 MILE)

1 **Dakota Swing (11+)** ★ Great route with good protection. The

direct start (5.12) takes the obvious fingercrack straight up to the dihedral. FA: Bob D'Antonio. Gear: To #2 Friend. FA: Bob D'Antonio and Brent Kertzman, 1984.

2 **Mind Games (11+ R)** ★ Hard moves with not so good protection. Gear: To #2.5 Friend. FA: Dale Goddard and Will Gadd, 1984.

3 **Secret Journey (9)** ★ Gear: To #3 Friend. FA: Brent Kertzman and Dave Bower, 1985.

THE SPRAY WALL (2.3 MILES)

1 **Spew (12+)** ★★ Excellent climbing up the overhanging arête. Gear: Quickdraws. FA: Darrly Roth, 1994.

2 **Rapture (13–)** ★★ Steep and strenuous. Gear: Quickdraws. FA: Dan Durland, 1994.

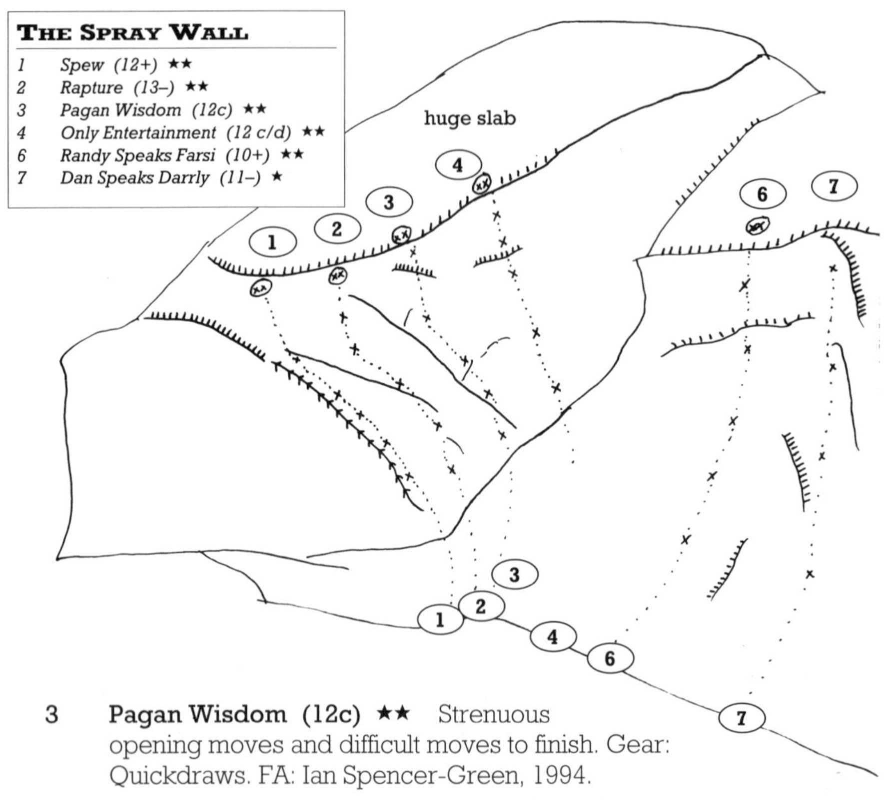

3 **Pagan Wisdom (12c) ★★** Strenuous opening moves and difficult moves to finish. Gear: Quickdraws. FA: Ian Spencer-Green, 1994.

4 **Only Entertainment (12 c/d) ★★** One of the best routes on the rock. Gear: Quickdraws. FA: Mike Johnson. First Redpoint Ascent: Ian Spencer-Green, 1994.

5 **Unknown (12)** Not quite the quality of the other routes. Gear: Quickdraws. FA: Unknown.

6 **Randy Speaks Farsi (10+) ★★** Great warmup route on big holds. Gear: Quickdraws. FA: Bill Schmauser, 1993.

7 **Dan Speaks Darrly (11–) ★** Gear: Quickdraws. FA: Dan Durland.

BIGOT ROCKS (2.6 MILES)

1 **The Arms Race (12–)** ★★ Great climbing out a 25-foot roof. Gear: To #2.5 Friend, Stoppers. FA: Bob D'Antonio, 1984.

2 **? (12+)** Start just right of the *Arms Race* up the overhanging wall. FA: Unknown.

3 **Will Power (12–)** ★ Good stemming up the obvious dihedral. Gear: RPs, small camming gear and wired Stoppers. FA: Neil Cannon, Bob D'Antonio and Will Gadd, 1983.

4 **Xenophobia (12c)** Gear: Quickdraws. FA: Darrly Roth, 1990.

5 **Just Do Me (12c)** Too close to the road, this route should have never been put in. Bolts have been pulled. FA: Unknown.

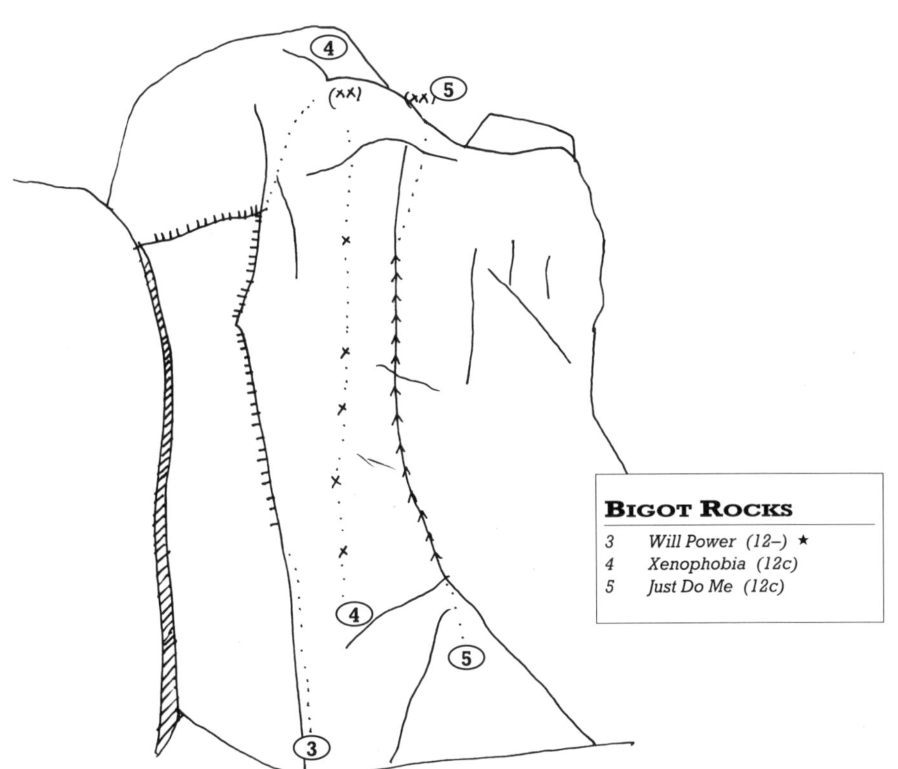

THE TOOTH

1 *Tooth Decay (8)*
2 *The Wound that Never Heals (9)*
3 *Novocaine (11+)* ★

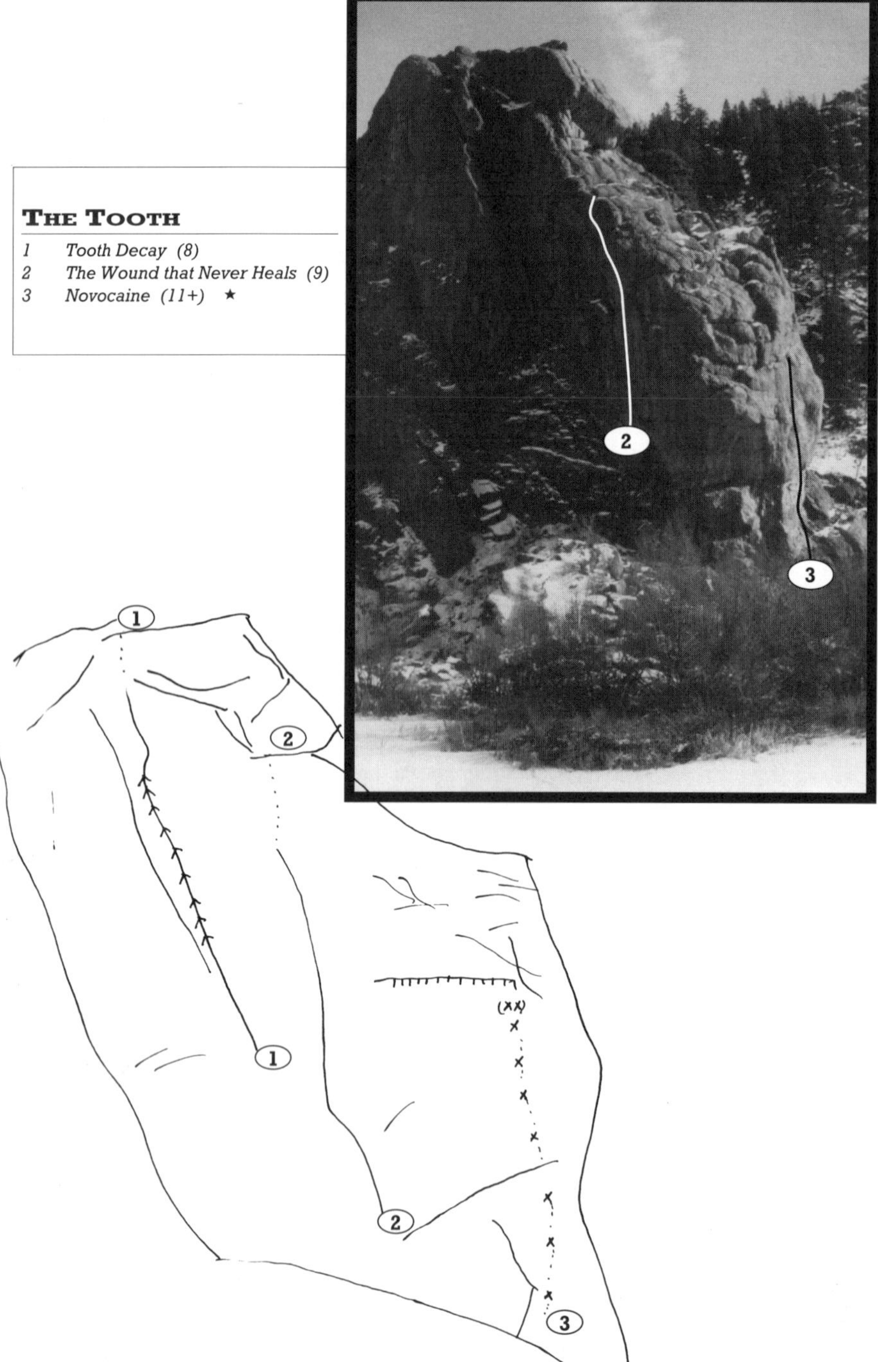

THE TOOTH (2.7 MILES)

1 **Tooth Decay (8)** Not the best-looking route in the canyon. Gear: To #3 Friend. FA: Unknown.

2 **The Wound that Never Heals (9)** This route takes the crack on the north-facing wall. Gear: To #3 Friend. FA: Andy Brown and Lotus Steele, 1983.

3 **Novocaine (11+) ★** A good looking route on the northwest face. Gear: #2.5 Friend, Quickdraws. FA:.

ELEVENMILE DOME (2.8 MILES)

Quality climbing on good rock, this long south-facing crag offers some of the more moderate routes in the canyon. Be prepared for the approach, it takes all of ten seconds. On most routes the difficult climbing ends after the first pitch, rap off or continue on easier rock to the top.

1 **Kathy's Crack (4)** Takes the low-angle crack on the west face. Gear: To #3 Friend. FA: Unknown.

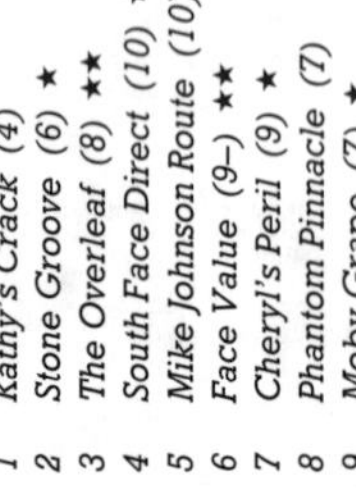

ELEVENMILE DOME

1 *Kathy's Crack* (4)
2 *Stone Groove* (6) ★
3 *The Overleaf* (8) ★★
4 *South Face Direct* (10) ★★★
5 *Mike Johnson Route* (10) ★
6 *Face Value* (9–) ★★
7 *Cheryl's Peril* (9) ★
8 *Phantom Pinnacle* (7)
9 *Moby Grape* (7) ★
10 *Original Sin* (9) ★★
11 *Jet Setter* (7) ★
12 *Happy Trails* (6) ★

2 **Stone Groove (6)** ★ Gear: Large Friends. FA: Unknown.

3 **The Overleaf (8)** ★★ Quality climbing on good rock with good protection. Gear: To #3.5 Friend. FA: Unknown.

4 **South Face Direct (10)** ★★★ The best route on the rock. Gear: Quickdraws. FA: Russ Johnson and John DeLong, 1982.

5 **Mike Johnson Route (10)** ★ Gear: Quickdraws. FA: Mike Johnson.

6 **Face Value (9–)** ★★ Quality climbing with long runouts. FA: Kevin Lindorff, Bob D'Antonio and Frank Hill, 1984.

7 **Cheryl's Peril (9)** ★ An excellent long pitch on good rock with adequate protection. Gear: Quickdraws. FA: Bryan Becker, 1978.

8 **Phantom Pinnacle (7)** Two-pitch route to base of summit overhang. Gear: Stoppers, Friends to #3. FA: Unknown.

9 **Moby Grape (7)** ★ Good route for learning how to place natural gear. Gear: To #2.5 Friend. FA: Unknown.

10 **Original Sin (9)** ★★ Good slab climbing to the obvious belay/rappel anchors. Gear: Small Stoppers, Quickdraws. FA: Stewart Green and Martha Morris, 1994.

11 **Jet Setter (7)** ★ Good traditional route with some runouts. Gear: Stoppers, small camming gear and medium Friends. FA: Stewart Green, Johnny Meyers and Ed Russell, 1979.

12 **Happy Trails (6)** ★ Goes up slab past six bolts to anchor. Gear: Small camming gear and Quickdraws. FA: Stewart Green, 1979.

13 **Ez Street (7)** ★ Gear: Stoppers and Quickdraws. FA: Stewart Green, Johnny Meyers and Ed Russell, 1979.

ARCH ROCK (4.0 MILES)

Arch Rock is by far one of the finest pieces of granite in the canyon. Arch Rock offers a lot of varied climbing with the routes ascending cracks, corners, roofs and slabs for two or three pitches to the top.

1 **The Staircase (5)** ★★★ One of the finest moderate routes in Colorado. Follow "The Staircase" on the left side of the rock. Gear: Stoppers,Friends to #3, Quickdraws and slings. FA: Unknown.

2 **Haircase (11–)** ★ After the first belay on *The Staircase* go left to the overhangs then up. Gear: To #2.5 Friends. FA: Andy Brown?

3 **Scarecase (10)** ★ First done by Bryan Becker without the bolts. Gear: To #2 Friends. FA: Bryan Becker, 1976.

4 **Kansas Honey (9)** Gear: To #2.5 Friend. FA: Leonard Coyne.

5 **Hollow Flake (6)** ★ Gear: To #3.5 Friend, slings and Stoppers. FA: Unknown.

6 **Sprout Route (11)** Could have better bolts. Gear: To #2.5 Friend, Stoppers and slings. FA: Leonard Coyne.

7 **Death by Drowning (10+)** ★ Excellent climbing with good protection and moves. Gear: To #2.5 Friend and Quickdraws. FA: Bob D'Antonio and Stewart Green, 1994.

8 **Captain Fist (8)** ★ Good route up the left side of the Tilted Tower. Gear: To #3 Friend. FA: Bryan Becker, 1976.

9 **The Meanie Cracks (7)** The obvious three cracks at the base of the Tilted Tower. Gear: Stoppers, Friends and hexes. FA: Unknown.

10 **Middle Dihedral (6)** ★ Takes the obvious dihedral up the center of the tower. FA: Brian Becker.

11 **Arch Rock Direct (7 R)** ★★ This is a good route up the face above the tower. It is 5.10 if you go over the roof at the top. Gear: To #2.5 Friend. FA: Bryan Becker, 1975.

12 **Village Idiot (9)** ★★ Starts on ledge 20 feet and climbs the slab of the tower. Gear: Stoppers, small camming gear and Quickdraws. FA: Stewart Green and Josh Morris, 1994.

13 **Zendance (7)** ★ Good face pitch with some runouts. Gear: Stoppers and Quickdraws. FA: Stewart Green and Ian Spencer-Green. First Solo: Bryan Becker.

14 **Obscura Direct (7)** ★★ Great route on the steep face right of Tilted Tower. Gear: Stoppers, small camming gear. FA: Bryan Becker, 1975.

15 **Arch Rock Route (8)** Gear: To #3.5 Friend. FA: Unknown.

EAGLE RIDGE (4.2 MILES)

This obscure cluster of rocks offers a couple of good routes with many new routes waiting to be done. The crags are located east and uphill from Turret Dome.

1 **Aerial Boundaries (12–)** ★★ Good fingercrack with excellent protection. Gear: To #2.5 Friend and RPs. FA: Darrly Roth and Kim Stiener, 1986.

2 **My Dog Could Have Died (11+ R)** ★ Hard moves and hard to place gear. Gear: To #2 Friend. FA: Bob D'Antonio and Brent Kertzman, 1984.

3 **Book with a Loose Binding (11–)** Climbs the obvious dihedral 100 feet right of My Dog. Gear: Quickdraws and Friends to #2. FA: Bob D'Antonio and Brent Kertzman, 1984.

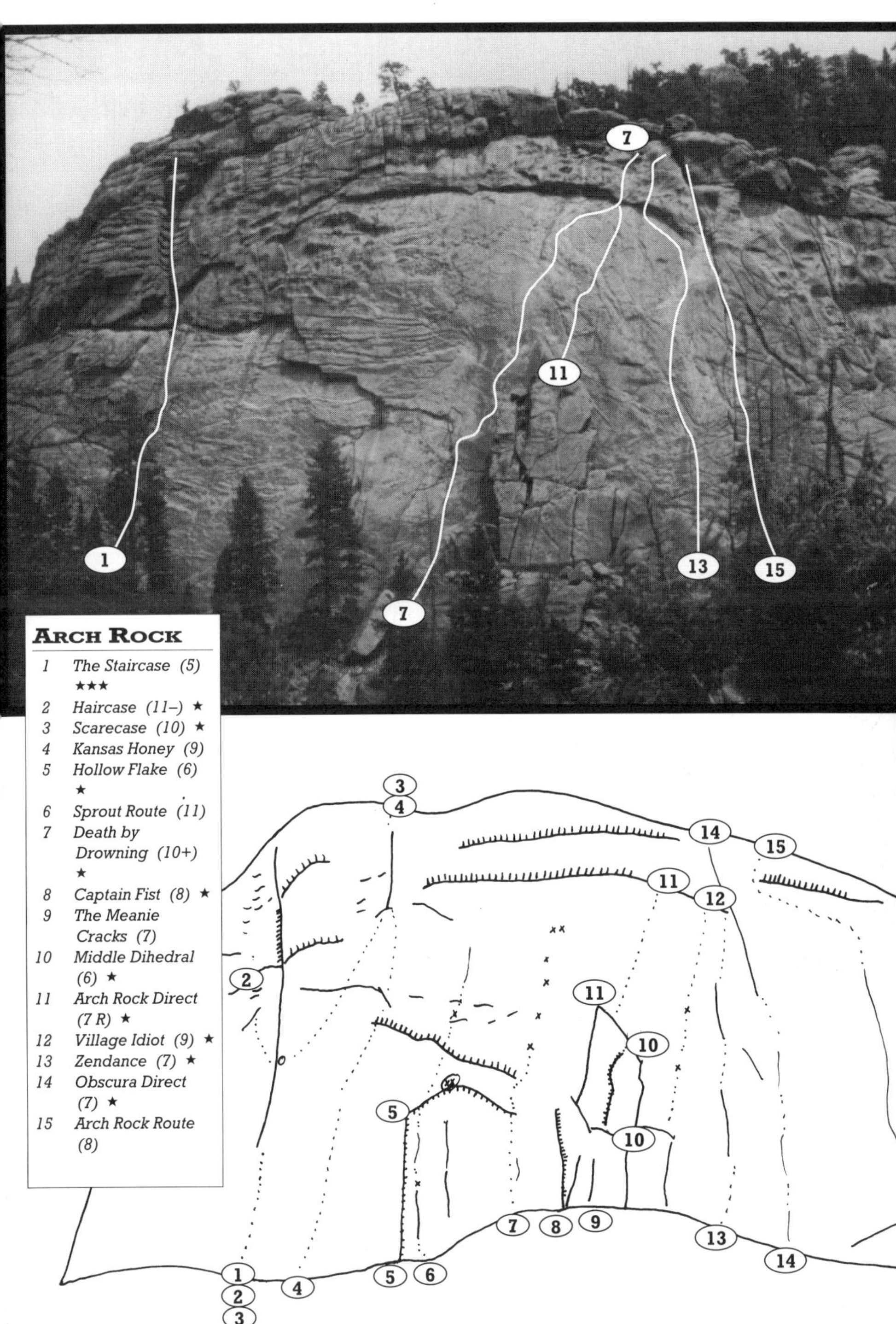

7
11
1
7
13
15
ARCH ROCK
1 The Staircase (5) ★★★
2 Haircase (11–) ★
3 Scarecase (10) ★
4 Kansas Honey (9)
5 Hollow Flake (6) ★
6 Sprout Route (11)
7 Death by Drowning (10+) ★
8 Captain Fist (8) ★
9 The Meanie Cracks (7)
10 Middle Dihedral (6) ★
11 Arch Rock Direct (7 R) ★
12 Village Idiot (9) ★
13 Zendance (7) ★
14 Obscura Direct (7) ★
15 Arch Rock Route (8)
3
4
14
15
11
12
2
11
10
5
10
7
8
9
13
14
1
2
3
4
5
6

TURRET DOME (4.3 MILES)

Turret Dome is the largest rock in Elevenmile and offers an excellent selection of moderate slab routes. The south face has routes up to three pitches with runouts in some places. The west face is shorter and offer steeper and few difficult routes.

1 **Inner Arch (9)** ★ Good climbing up the face leading to the obvious arch. Gear: Quickdraws and Stoppers. FA: Unknown.

2 **White Stress (12–)** ★★★ One of the best face routes in the canyon. Do it. Gear: Small camming gear, RPs and Quickdraws. FA: Bob D'Antonio and Neil Cannon, 1985.

3 **Aid Route (9+)** ★★ Excellent crack climbing with good protection. Gear: To #3 Friend. FA: Peter Williams and Peter Gallagher, 1979.

4 **Test Pattern (10+)** ★ Same start as *Aid Route*. Go right after ten feet. Gear: To #2.5 Friend. FA: Unknown.

5 **Balls, Balls (11c R)** Somewhat runout. Gear: To #2 Friend and small camming gear. FA: Darrly Roth, 1985.

6 **Guide's Route (6)** ★★ Good beginner route. Gear: To #3 Friend. FA: Unknown.

7 **Schooldaze (5)** ★★ Another great beginner route with excellent protection. Gear: To #3.5 Friend. FA: Unknown.

8 **Phace Route (6)** ★ The second pitch takes you up to the bathtubs. Gear: To #3 Friend. FA: Unknown.

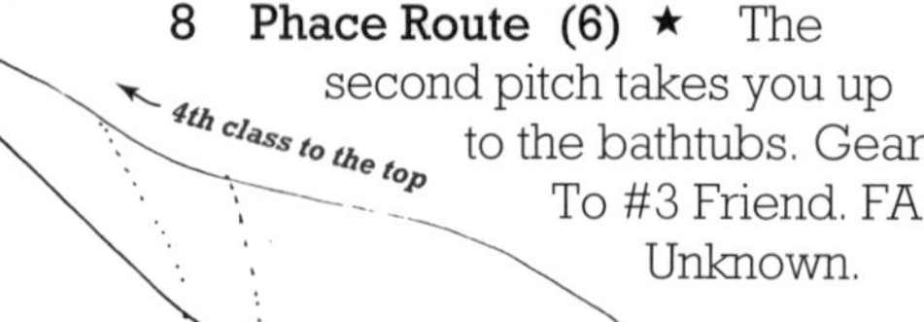

TURRET DOME

1 *Inner Arch (9)* ★
2 *White Stress (12–)* ★★★
3 *Aid Route (9+)* ★★
4 *Test Pattern (10+)* ★
7 *Schooldaze (5)* ★★
8 *Phace Route (6)* ★
9 *Jaws (5)* ★
10 *The Worm (8)* ★
11 *Fishhook (5)*
12 *Upper Lip (7)* ★★

9 **Jaws (5) ★** This route follow the obvious left-facing arch on the southwest face. Gear: To #4 Friend. FA: Unknown.

10 **The Worm (8) ★** Great one-pitch route, rappel from the trees. Gear: To #3 Friend. FA: Unknown.

11 **Fishhook (5)** Follow the obvious right-facing arch just right of *The Worm*. You need two ropes to rappel from the trees. Gear: To #3.5 Friend. FA: Unknown.

12 **Upper Lip (7) ★★** Takes the obvious crack above the bathtubs to the summit. Gear: Medium Friends and Stoppers. FA: Unknown.

13 **Sunshine Face (0)** This low-angle slab is perfect for beginners. Gear: Stoppers, Friends and Quickdraws. FA: Unknown.

HARD ROCK (4.7 MILES)

This hidden gem has three exceptional routes well worth the approach. The best way to approach Hard Rock is from the Springer Gulch Campground. Walk past Teale Tower to the Sports Crag then north uphill to the rock.

1 **I Engineer (11c) ★★** Climbs the left-slanting crack on the left side of the crag. Gear: Small camming gear, Stoppers and Quickdraws. FA: Bob D'Antonio, 1984.

2 **Reach for the Sky (11c) ★★** Good steep jug hauling! Gear: Stoppers and small camming gear. FA: Dale Goddard and Bob D'Antonio, 1984.

3 **King for a Day (12c) ★★★** One of the canyon's best short hard routes. Gear: Quickdraws, small camming gear and Stoppers. FA: Bob D'Antonio and Dale Goddard, 1984.

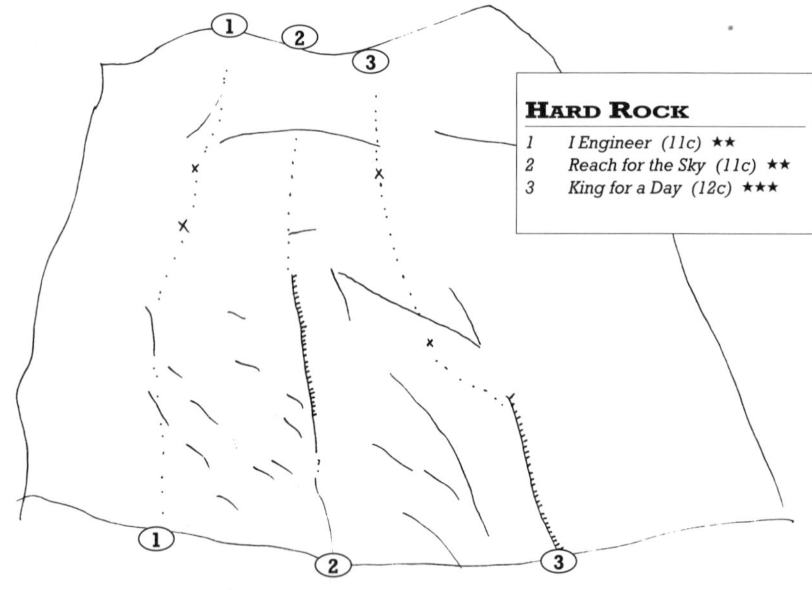

SPORTS CRAG (5.1 MILES)

For such a small crag, this crag packs a powerful punch. It offers a high concentration of hard routes. Most routes end on a ledge halfway up the wall. Walk off to the east.

1 **Ecstasy and Wiseguys (11c R) ★★** Some sport climbing dickweed added four bolts to this route after the first ascent. This is a prime example of how pathetic some climbers are! The bolts have been removed. Gear: Stoppers and small camming gear. FA: Bob D'Antonio and Peter Gallagher, 1982.

2 **Moonage Daydreaming (12) ★★** Very technical stemming up a blank corner. Gear: Quickdraws and medium Friends. FA: Mark Rolofson and Bob D'Antonio, 1983.

3 **Albatross (12c) ★★** Painful finger jamming up a thin crack, very continuous. Gear: To #2 Friends. FFA: Chris Peisker, 1982.

4 **Shock the Monkey (12–) ★★** Good hand jams out a 20-foot roof. Gear: To #2.5 Friend. FA: Bob D'Antonio and Mark Rolofson, 1982.

5 **Fiddler Under the Roof (11–) ★★** Traverse right under the *Shock the Monkey* roof past two pins. Gear: Quickdraws, Friends and small camming gear. FA: Russ Johnson and John Delong, 1981.

6 **Desmond Dynamo (12–) ★★** Excellent overhanging climbing with good protection, if you can hang on to place it. Gear: To #2.5 Friend. FA: Bob D'Antonio, Frank Hill and Kevin Lindorff, 1984.

7 **The Leaner (10) ★★** Great route, do it. Gear: To #2 Friend. FA: Russ Johnson and John DeLong, 1982.

8 **Trout Fishing in America (8) ★** Long name for such a short route. Gear: Stoppers and small cams. FA: Bob D'Antonio solo, 1983.

9 **Warmup Corner (8) ★** Gear: To #2.5 Friend. FA: Russ Johnson and John DeLong, 1982.

10 **Concrete Slippers (11- R) ★★** The crux is well protected, it's just the runout to the second bolt that will kill you. FA: Kevin Lindorff, Bob D'Antonio and Frank Hill, 1984.

SPORTS CRAG

1 Ecstasy and Wiseguys (11c R) ★★
2 Moonage Daydreaming (12) ★★
3 Albatross (12c) ★★
4 Shock the Monkey (12–) ★★
5 Fiddler Under the Roof (11–) ★★
6 Desmond Dynamo (12–) ★★
7 The Leaner (10) ★★
8 Trout Fishing in America (8) ★
9 Warmup Corner (8) ★
10 Concrete Slippers (11- R) ★★

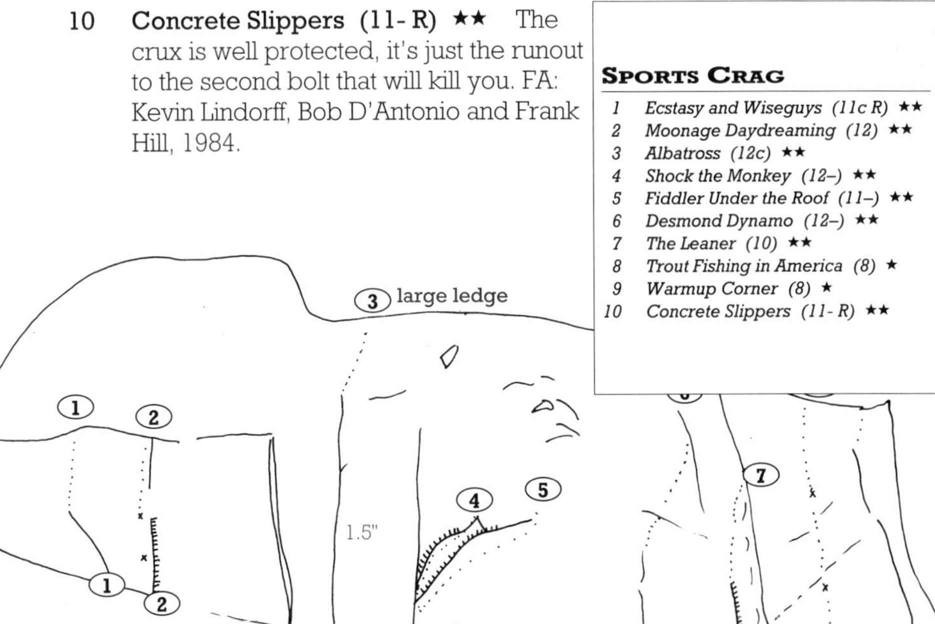

TEALE TOWER (5.2 MILES)

This beautiful piece of granite has one the best routes in all of Elevenmile, this is a must stop for the visiting climber.

1 **Unknown (11)** Obvious wide crack left of Teale Tower Route. Gear: To #4 Friend. FA: Unknown.

2 **Teale Tower Route (11–) ★★★** An Elevenmile classic. This route is a must do for any climber visiting Elevenmile. Gear: Stoppers, Friends to #3 Friends and slings. FA: Peter Gallagher and Peter Williams, 1979.

3 **Run for Your Life (11- R) ★** You can run but you can't hide. Somewhat runout in the corner. Gear: Stoppers, Friends, small camming gear and slings. FA: Richard Aschert and Darrly Roth, 1984.

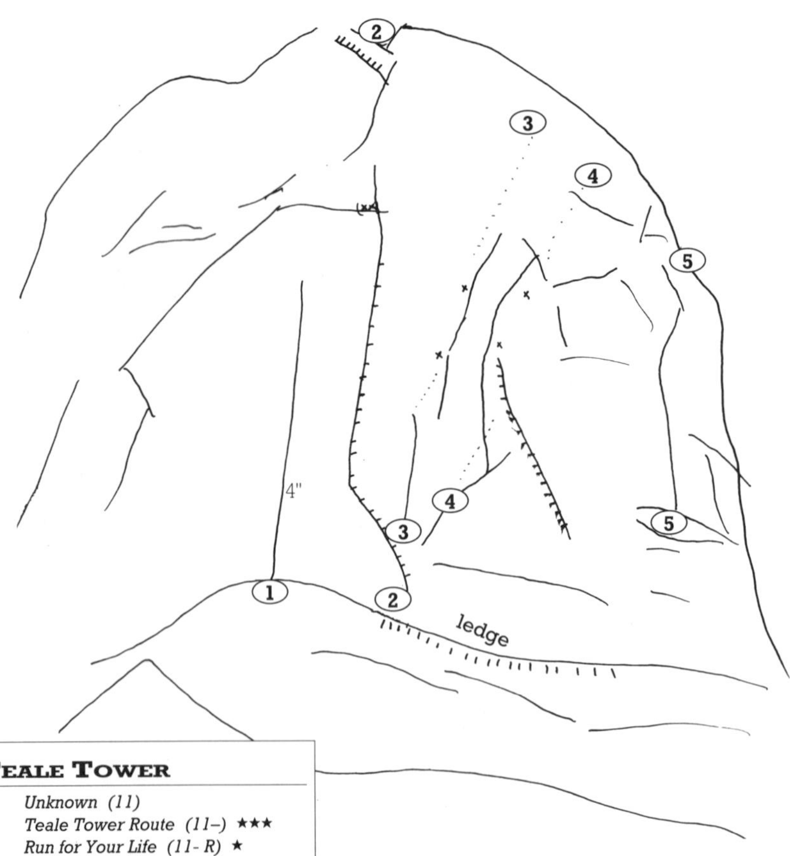

TEALE TOWER

1 Unknown (11)
2 Teale Tower Route (11–) ★★★
3 Run for Your Life (11- R) ★
4 Candidate for Space (11 R) ★★
5 Reality Check (10+) ★

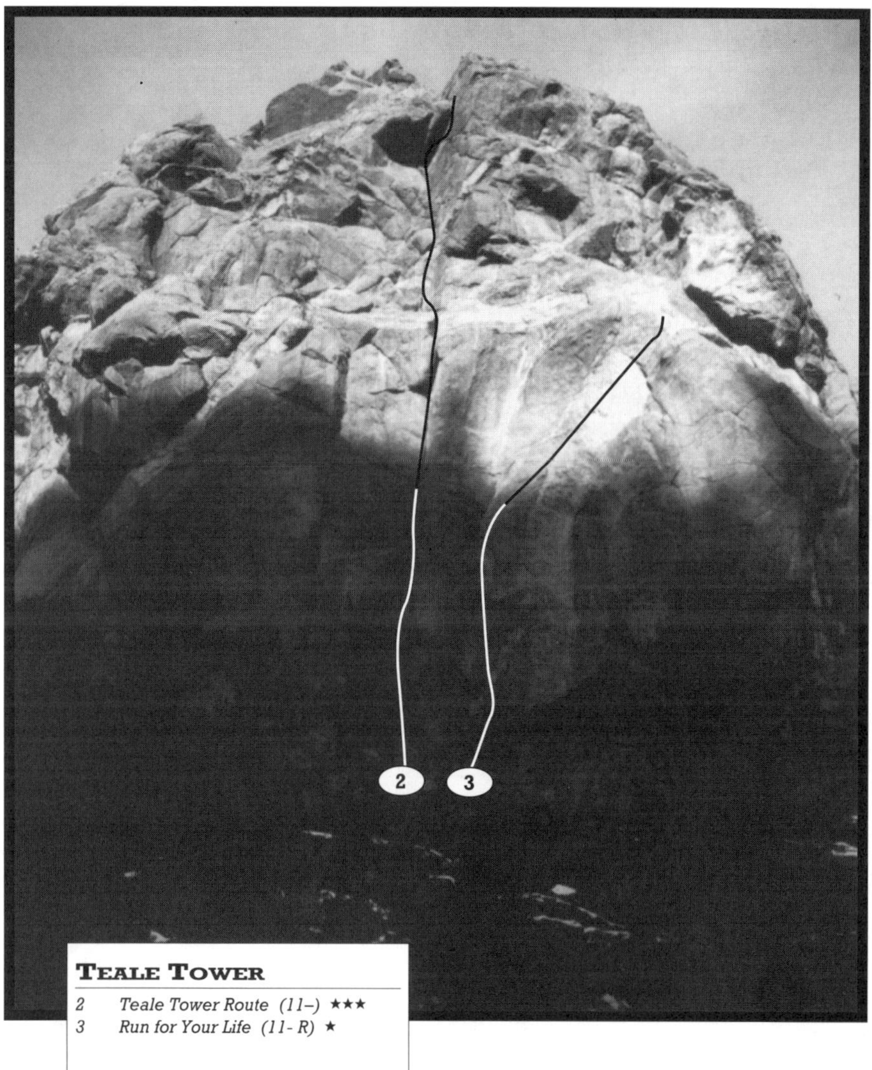

TEALE TOWER

2 Teale Tower Route (11–) ★★★

3 Run for Your Life (11- R) ★

4 **Candidate for Space (11 R)** ★★ A fall on this route and that's what you'll be. Gear: RPs, small camming gear, Friends and slings. FA: Dale Goddard and Brent Kertzman, 1984.

5 **Reality Check (10+)** ★ Good climbing, do it. Gear: Friends to #3, Stoppers and small cams. FA: Darrly Roth and Kim Steiner, 1983.

SPRINGER GULCH (5.4 MILES)

Excellent routes, good rock and a variety of climbs, make this crag a must stop for any climber visiting Elevenmile Canyon.

1 **Here's Two Old Fools (11+)** No fool like an old fool. Gear: Rack to #2 Friend. FA: Rick Westbay and Mark Milligan, 1986.

2 **Statement for Youth (12–) ★★** A little bat shit should not keep you off this excellent route. Gear: Rack To #2 Friend. FA: Bob D'Antonio and Richard Aschert, 1986.

3 **Little Kingdom (13) ★★** Hardest technical route in the area. Gear: Quickdraws. FA: Bob D'Antonio, 1986.

4 **Here's to Old Flakes (11) ★** Gear: Rack to #2.5 Friend. FA: Mark Milligan, 1986.

5 **Here's to Future Ways (12) ★★★** The first and the best of the *Here's to* ... routes. Great route with the crux at the top. Gear: Medium Friends, Stoppers and Quickdraws. FA: Bob D'Antonio.

6 **Stolen Torque (11) ★** More like a boulder problem. Gear: Small camming gear. FA: Brent Kertzman, 1985.

7 **Cries and Whimpers (10)** Starts about 50 feet left of the Intimidator. Gear: To #2.5 Friend. FA: Mark Milligan, 1986.

8 **The Intimidator (12+) ★★** Excellent and difficult crack climbing out a roof. Gear: Stoppers, small cams and Friends. FA: Mark Milligan, 1986.

9 **Kevin Route (12+) ★★** Gear: Stoppers, Friends and Quickdraws. FA: Kevin McLaughlin and Glen Schuler, 1993.

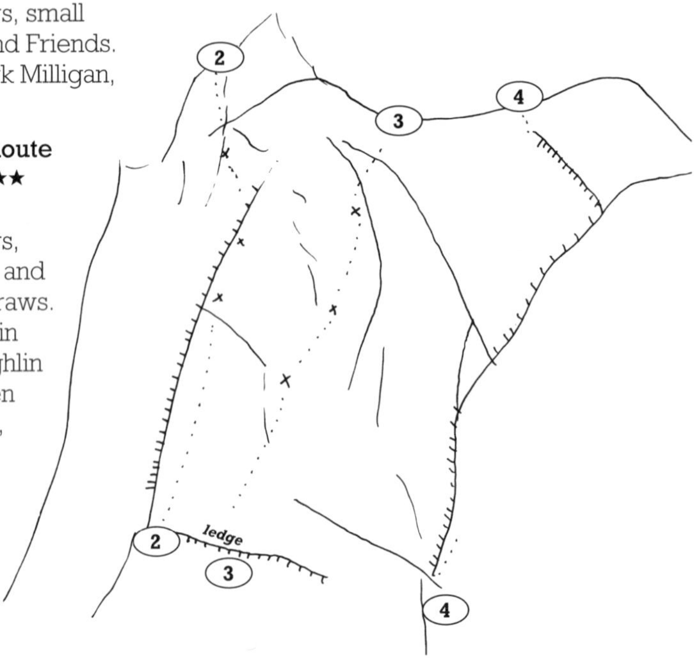

10 **Surfing with an Alien (11+) ★★★** Classic face climb, do it. Gear: Quickdraws. FA: Glen Schuler, 1992.

11 **Overpower by Funk (12+) ★★** Hard moves to start, pumping moves to the top. Gear: Quickdraws and a #1.5 Friend. FA: Glen Schuler and Kevin McLaughlin, 1993.

12 **Sunkist (7) ★** Good mid-range route. Gear: Quickdraws FA: Glen and Judy Schuler, 1992.

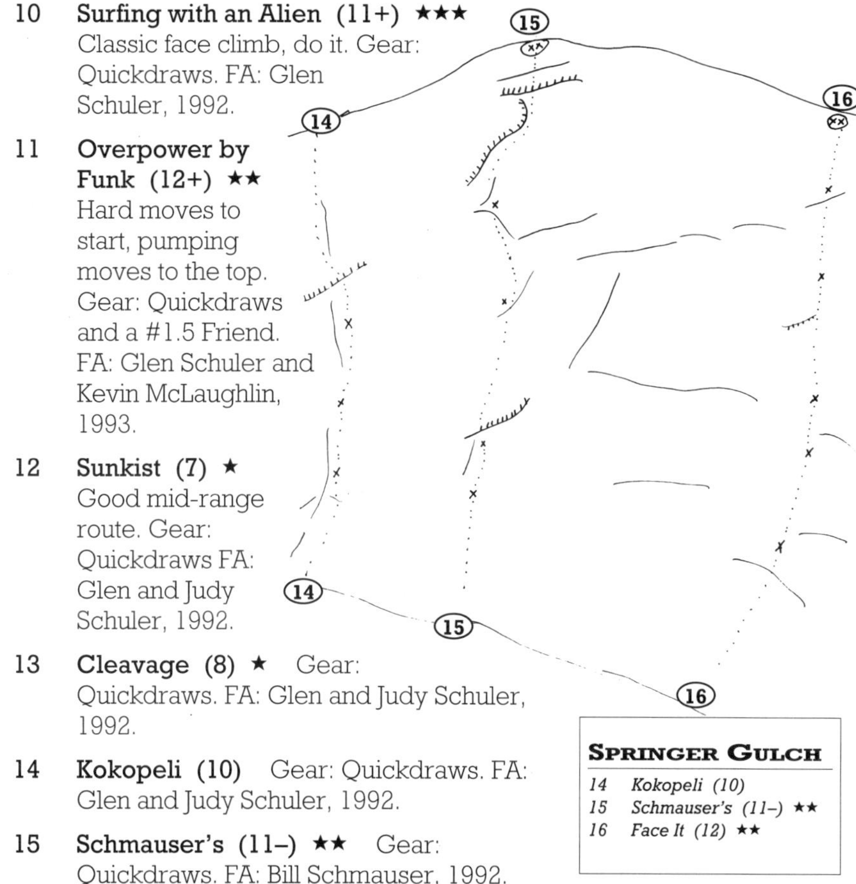

13 **Cleavage (8) ★** Gear: Quickdraws. FA: Glen and Judy Schuler, 1992.

14 **Kokopeli (10)** Gear: Quickdraws. FA: Glen and Judy Schuler, 1992.

15 **Schmauser's (11–) ★★** Gear: Quickdraws. FA: Bill Schmauser, 1992.

SPRINGER GULCH

14 Kokopeli (10)
15 Schmauser's (11–) ★★
16 Face It (12) ★★

16 **Face It (12) ★★** Easy to face, hard to do. Gear: Quickdraws. FA: Mark Milligan, 1993.

About 200 yards up and right of Face It is the Scoop Wall. See topo on page 36.

17 **Crest of a Wave (10+) ★** Gear: Stoppers and small to medium Friends. FA: Mark Milligan and Ricky Westbay, 1991.

18 **Body English (11–) ★★** Good climbing on excellent rock. Gear: Quickdraws and small to medium Friends. FA: Glen Schuler, 1992.

19 **Scoop DeVille (10+) ★★★** One of the best 5.10s at Elevenmile Canyon. Gear: Quickdraws. FA: Glen Schuler, 1992.

20 **English Body (9)** Gear: Stoppers and Quickdraws. FA: Mark Milligan, 1992.

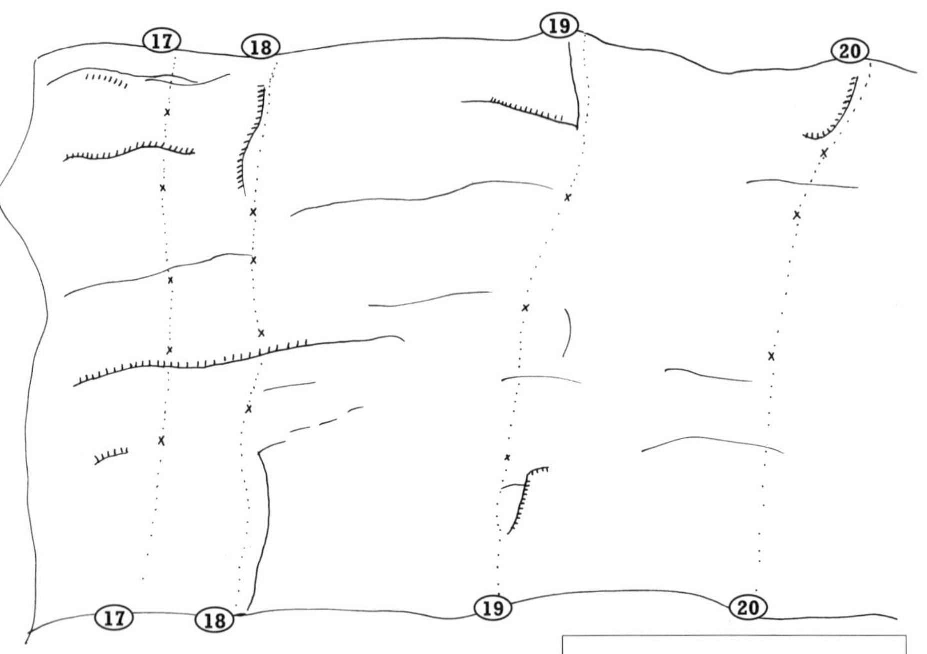

SPRINGER GULCH–SCOOP WALL

17 *Crest of a Wave (10+)* ★
18 *Body English (11–)* ★★
19 *Scoop DeVille (10+)* ★★★
20 *English Body (9)*

RIVER WALL (6.3 MILES)

Another excellent short crag with a variety of worthwhile routes. Great place to swim and jump off the boulders into the river in the summer.

1 **Lews Route (B1–)** On the far left side, up a short gully is this long boulder problem. FA: Bob D'Antonio, 1984.

2 **Wingless Angel (11)** Ten feet left of Captain Cod Peice is this long boulder problem. FA: Bob D'Antonio, 1984.

3 **Captain Cod Peice (11) ★★** Deceiving crack climbing up a steep wall. Gear: Stoppers, small cams and medium Friends. FA: Bob D'Antonio, Frank Hill and Kevin Lindorff, 1984.

4 **Darylect (12) ★★** Good steep climbing! Gear: Quickdraws. FA: Ian Spencer-Green and Bob D'Antonio, 1994.

5 **Simple Minds (12) ★** Gear: Medium Friends and Quickdraws. FA: Bob D'Antonio and Richard Aschert, 1985.

6 **Loaf and Jug (7) ★** Gear: To #2 Friend. FA: Stewart Green and Martha Morris, 1994.

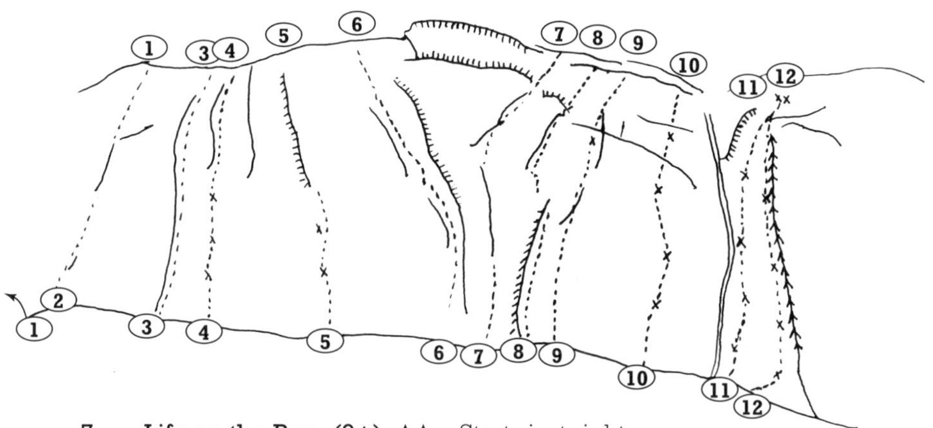

7 **Life on the Run (9+) ★★** Starts just right of the huge roof. Gear: To #2 Friend. FA: Bob D'Antonio and Mark Heese, 1985.

8 **Running Man (9 R) ★** Gear: RPs, Stopper and small cams. FA: Bob D'Antonio and Mark Heese, 1985.

9 **Blood Brothers (12) ★★** Hard moves over the bulge. Gear: Medium Friends, Stoppers and Quickdraws. FA: Bob D'Antonio and Ian Spencer-Green, 1994.

10 **Flat Earth Society (11) ★★** Gear: Quickdraws. FA: Ian Spencer-Green and Stewart Green, 1995.

RIVER WALL

1 *Lews Route (B1–)*
2 *Wingless Angel (11)*
3 *Captain Cod Peice (11) ★★*
4 *Darylect (12) ★★*
5 *Simple Minds (12) ★*
6 *Loaf and Jug (7) ★*
7 *Life on the Run (9+) ★★*
8 *Running Man (9 R) ★*
9 *Blood Brothers (12) ★★*
10 *Flat Earth Society (11) ★★*
11 *Pumping Chuck (11) ★*
12 *Skid Marks (11) ★★★*

11 **Pumping Chuck (11) ★** A little scaly but still a good route. Gear: Quickdraws. FA: Bob D'Antonio and Chuck Carlson, 1994.

12 **Skid Marks (11) ★★★** A great arête climb with good position. Gear: Quickdraws. FA: Bob D'Antonio, Kevin Lindorff and Frank Hill, 1984.

SHORT WALL (6.7 MILES)

See topo on page 38.

1 **O.D. (10) ★** Watch out for the loose flake. Gear: Rack to #2 Friend. FA: Bob D'Antonio, 1984.

2 **Race with a Demon (11–) ★★** Excellent crack climbing up a steep wall. Gear: Rack to #2.5 Friend. FA: Bob D'Antonio and Shawn Wilson, 1983.

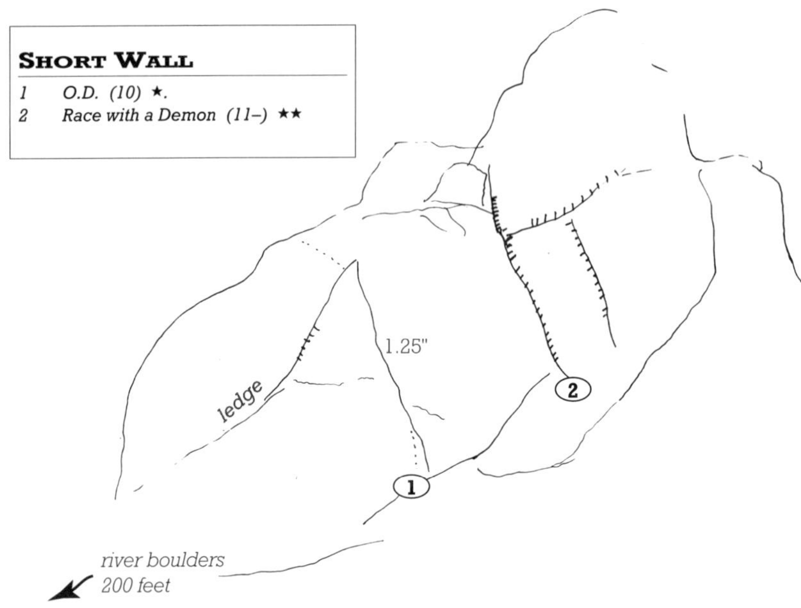

The next two climbs are located on a block 100 yards up the stream from the Short Wall.

3 **Bruised but not Battered (12) ★★** The right one of the two cracks. Gear: RPs, small cams and small Friends. FA: Bob D'Antonio and Chris Hill, 1983.

4 **The Last Farewell (11+) ★** Short and hard. Gear: RPs and small camming gear. FA: Bob D'Antonio, 1985.

The boulders right below the Short Wall have some of the best granite bouldering in the area. The east boulder has a number of excellent problems with the West Face (B1) being a classic. Most of the problems here were done by Harrison Dekker, Bob D'Antonio and Bob Murray.

SPY ROCK (6.9 MILES)

1 **Tesuque (10+) ★★** Good crack climbing to short runout face. Gear: To #2.5 Friend. FA: Bob D'Antonio.

2 **Spy vs Spy (12) ★★** Finger jamming out a tiered roof is the main attraction here. Gear: Small cams, Stoppers and Quickdraws. FA: Will Gadd and Eric Harp, 1985.

3 **Eric's Face (8)** Gear: To #2 Friend. FA: Eric Harp, 1985.

There is excellent bouldering up the hill and west of Spy Rock. Most of the problems are the work of Bob Murray, Mark Milligan, Kevin McLaughlin and Bob D'Antonio.

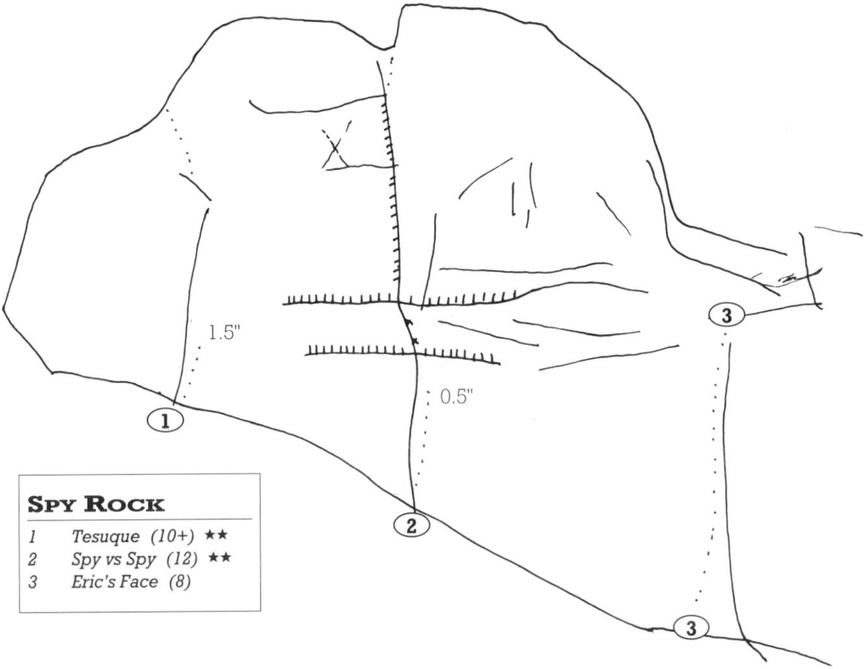

1.5"

0.5"

1

2

3

3

Spy Rock

1	*Tesuque (10+)*	★★
2	*Spy vs Spy (12)*	★★
3	*Eric's Face (8)*	

1

2

Spy Rock

1	*Tesuque (10+)*	★★
2	*Spy vs Spy (12)*	★★

INDULGENCE CRAG (7.0 MILES)

With a plethora of excellent routes this crag is by far one of the best in Elevenmile for the visiting Hardperson. With a high concentration of hard routes you have to be able to crank here. The routes require natural protection, so be prepared to place all the latest technology you have. The crag faces south and gets good sun in the fall and winter.

1 **The Slinger (9+) ★★** Good thin crack climbing on the far left side of the cliff. Gear: To #2.5 Friend. FA: Bob D'Antonio and Neil Cannon, 1985.

2 **Small Offering (12–) ★★** Short and sweet. Gear: Quickdraws and small cams. FA: Bob D'Antonio and Dale Goddard, 1985.

3 **The Sanctuary (12c R) ★★** With hard to place protection and hard moves this route will keep you on your toes. Gear: RPs, Stoppers, small cams and medium Friends. FA: Neil Cannon and Bob D'Antonio, 1985.

4 **The Holding Hand (12) ★★** Hard jams out and over the roof. Gear: To #2.5 Friend. FA: Dale Goddard and Bob D'Antonio, 1985.

5 **Catholic Girls (11–) ★★** Switching cracks is the crux. Gear: To #2.5 Friend. Bob D'Antonio, Dale Goddard and Will Gadd, 1984.

6 **Way Stoned and Snarling (11) ★★** Gear: To #3.5 Friend. FA: Mark Rolofson and Shawn Wilson, 1982.

7 **The Vatican (12) ★★** Excellent thin crack climbing up a vertical wall. Gear: RPs, small cams and small Friends. FA: Dale Goddard, Bob D'Antonio and Will Gadd, 1985.

INDULGENCE CRAG

1 *The Slinger (9+) ★★*
2 *Small Offering (12–) ★★*
3 *The Sanctuary (12c R) ★★*
4 *The Holding Hand (12) ★★*
5 *Catholic Girls (11–) ★★*
6 *Way Stoned and Snarling (11) ★★*
7 *The Vatican (12) ★★*

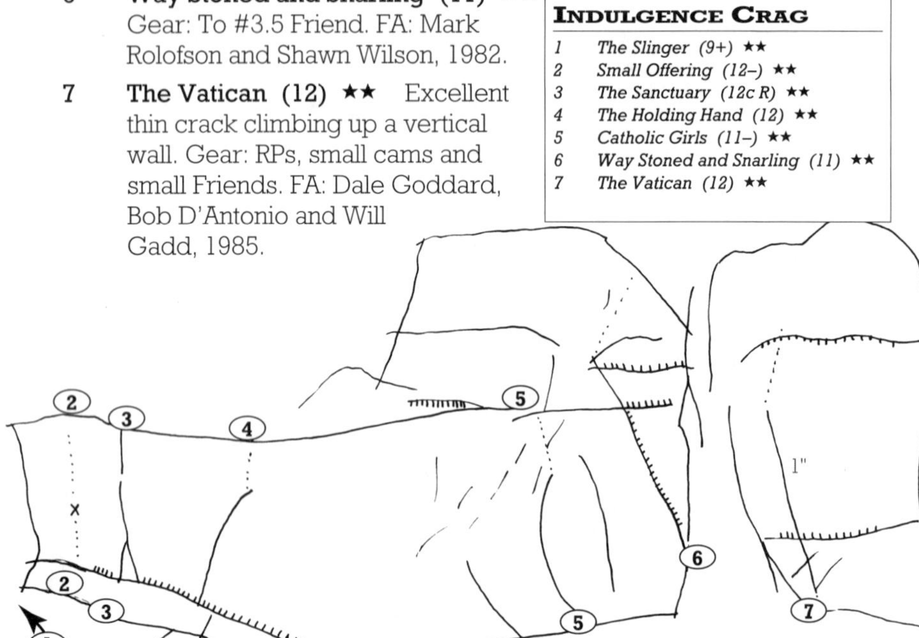

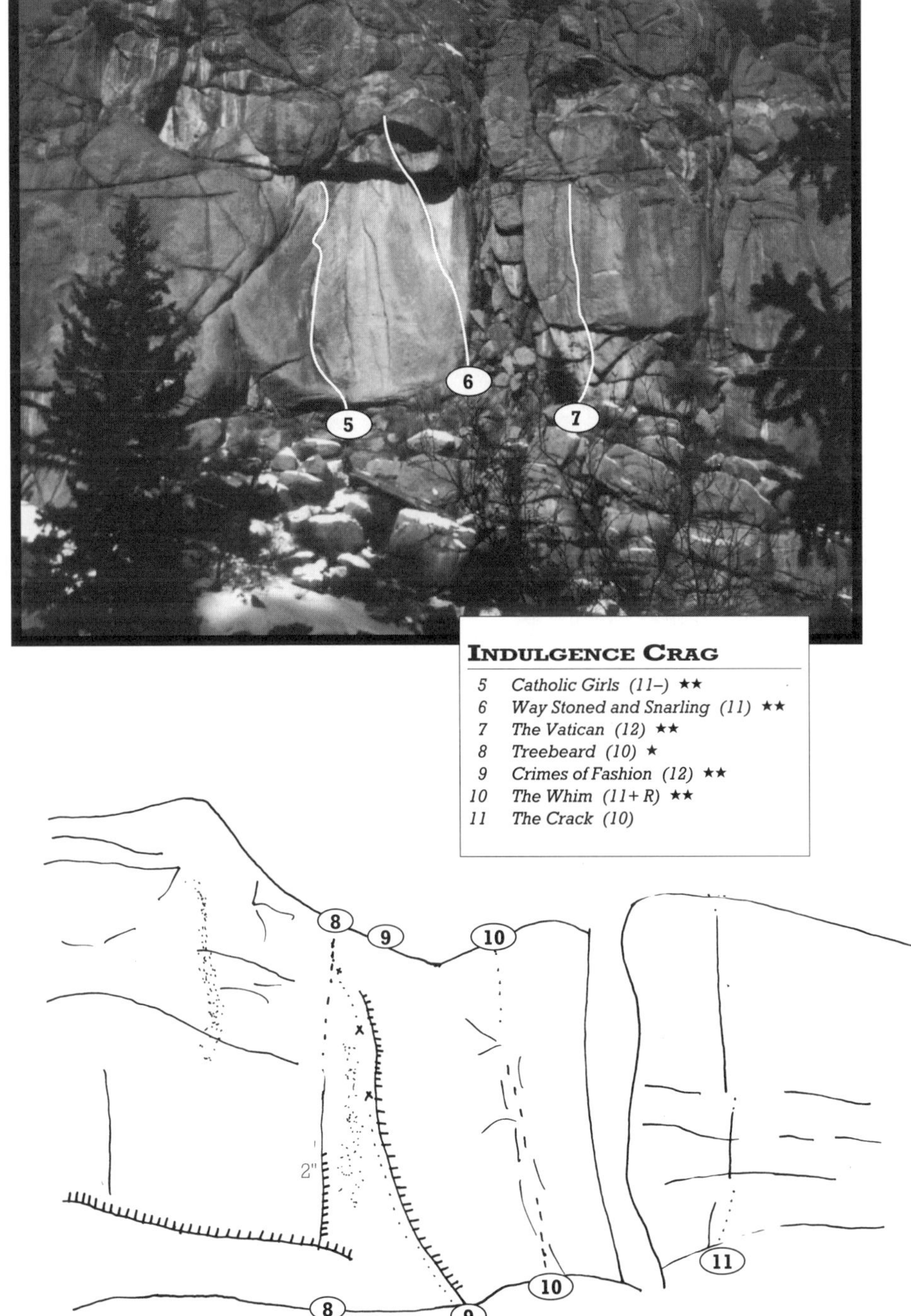

INDULGENCE CRAG

5 *Catholic Girls (11–)* ★★
6 *Way Stoned and Snarling (11)* ★★
7 *The Vatican (12)* ★★
8 *Treebeard (10)* ★
9 *Crimes of Fashion (12)* ★★
10 *The Whim (11+ R)* ★★
11 *The Crack (10)*

8 **Treebeard (10)** ★ Gear: To #3 Friend. FA: Kevin Murray and Steve Cheyney, 1980.

9 **Crimes of Fashion (12)** ★★ Hard stemming and laybacking up a thin left-facing corner. Gear: RPs, small cams, medium Friends and Quickdraws. FA: Mark Rolofson and Bob D'Antonio, 1982.

10 **The Whim (11+ R)** ★★ Hard climbing and difficult to place gear make for a serious route. Gear: Rack to #2 Friend. FA: Bob D'Antonio and Dale Goddard, 1984.

11 **The Crack (10)** Gear: To #3 Friend. FA: Unknown.

COVE ROCK (8.1 MILES)

With one of the best fingercracks in the area, easy access and west-facing exposure, this crag should be on any visiting climber's hit list.

1 **Zest (11)** The obvious crack to a face right off the road in the campground 200 yards west of Cove Rock. Gear: to #2 Friend. FA: Dale Goddard and Brent Kertzman, 1985.

2 **Face with a View (B1)** Almost long enough to be a route. FA: Bob D'Antonio.

3 **Chicago Blues (11c)** ★★ Great climbing with good protection at the hard moves. FA: Bob D'Antonio and Chuck Carlson, 1994.

4 **Neither Wolf nor Dog (12)** ★★ Gear: Quickdraws and a #2 Friend. FA: Bob D'Antonio and Chuck Carlson.

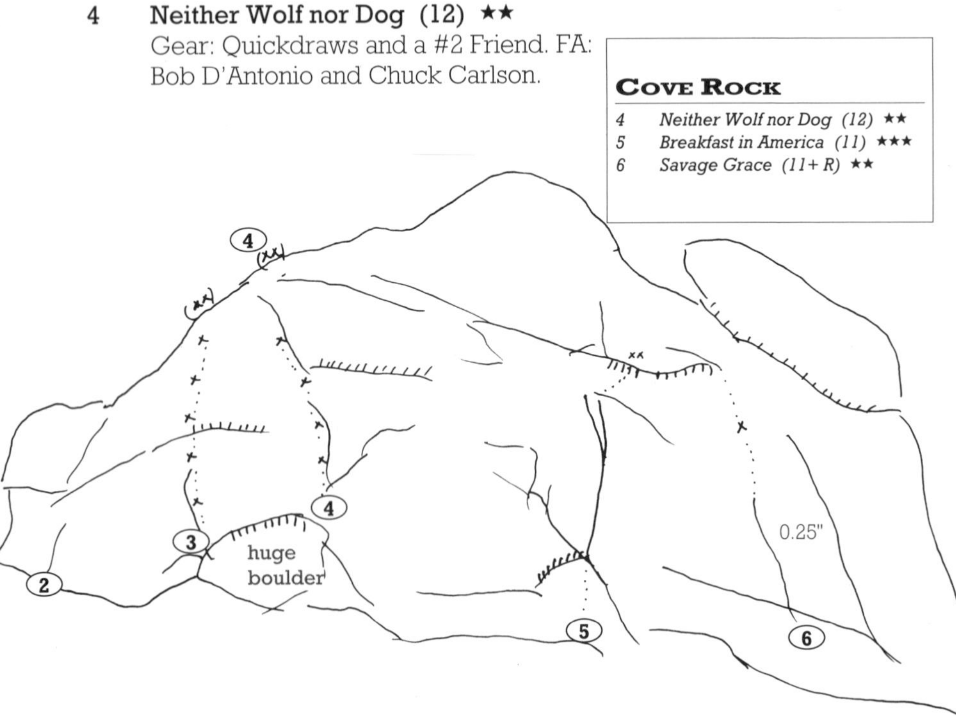

5 **Breakfast in America (11) ★★★** Classic, this is a must-do route. Gear: Wired Stoppers, small cams and medium Friends. FA: Bob D' Antonio, Pete O'Donovan and Alec Sharp, 1981.

6 **Savage Grace (11+ R) ★★** Serious climbing getting to the bolt. Gear: RPs small Stoppers and small cams. FA: Bob D'Antonio and Will Gadd, 1984.

7 **Genetic Imbalance (12–) ★** This route is located 300 yards downstream behind Cove Rock. Gear: Small cams and Quickdraws. FA: Bob D'Antonio and Richard Aschert, 1985.

PINE CONE DOME (8.2 MILES)

Another great crag with moderate routes and a short approach, good choice for climbers just getting into leading.

1 **Neck Row Feel Ya (10 R)** A little necky in places. Gear: Rack to #2.5 Friend. FA: Unknown.

2 **Anorexic Lycra Dog (12–) ★** Good hard face climbing to an anchor just below the roof. Gear: Quickdraws. FA: Unknown.

3 **Roof Bypass (6) ★** Good moderate climbing on excellent rock. Gear: Rack to #3 Friend. FA: Unknown.

PINE CONE DOME
2 Anorexic Lycra Dog (12–) ★
3 Roof Bypass (6) ★
4 Lichen or Leave It (9) ★
5 Ben Dover (9) ★★
6 Stone Age (5) ★★
7 Armaj Das (5) ★
8 Parr Four (10) ★
9 Pine Away (7) ★
walk off
xx
xx
2
3
4
5
6
7
8
9

4 **Lichen or Leave It (9)** ★ Gear: Rack to #3 Friend. FA: Unknown.

5 **Ben Dover (9)** ★★ Excellent face climbing to a double-bolt anchor. Gear: Quickdraws. FA: Unknown.

6 **Stone Age (5)** ★★ Gear: Rack to #3.5 Friend. FA: Unknown.

7 **Armaj Das (5)** ★ Gear: Rack to #3 Friend. FA: Unknown.

8 **Parr Four (10)** ★ Good climbing up the discontinuous cracks and slabs just right of Armaj Das. Gear: Rack to #3 Friend. FA: Unknown.

9 **Pine Away (7)** ★ Up the slab on the right side of the rock to a belay at the obvious tree. Gear: Rack to #2 Friend. FA: Stewart Green, Martha Morris and Dennis Jackson, 1990.

IDLEWILD PICNIC AREA (8.4 MILES)

This small group of rocks and crags has some excellent short routes with potential for a number of new routes on quality granite with a short approach.

1 **5.8 Corner (8)** ★ Follow the shallow crack in the left facing dihedral. Gear: Rack to #2.5 Friend. FA: Brent Kertzman and Mark Milligan, 1985.

2 **Squatter's Rights (11+)** ★ Hard moves getting over the roof. Gear: To #3 Friend. FA: Bob D'Antonio, 1985.

3 **Stemulation (10–)** ★★ Excellent stemming with hard moves at the top. Gear: Rack to #2.5 Friend. FA: Brent Kertzman and Mark Milligan, 1985.

EAST IDLEWILD ROCK

4 **Golden Dreams (12–)** ★★ Excellent face moves past two bolts to a right-leaning crack. Gear: Rack to #2 Friend. FA: Bob D'Antonio, 1984.

5 **Jet (10)** Short overhanging crack 30 feet right of Golden Dreams. Gear: To #2.5 Friend. FA: Mark Milligan and Rick Westbay.

6 **Bad Dreams (10)** Up and right of Jet is a short overhanging corner. Gear: To #3 Friend. FA: Bob D'Antonio and Mark Milligan, 1984.

WEST IDLEWILD ROCK

7 **Dale Solo (10+)** Gear: To #2.5 Friend. FA: Dale Goddard and Bob D'Antonio solo, 1984.

8 **Escape From Alabama (11+)** ★★ Up short corner to face with two bolts. Good route, do it. Gear: To #2 Friend. FA: Bob D'Antonio, Dale Goddard and Gene Smith, 1986.

9 **Rubber Soul (12–)** ★★ Hard face moves to gain the crack, excellent route. Gear: Quickdraws and small Aliens. FA: Bob D'Antonio and Chuck Carlson, 1994.

BABOON ROCK
3 Fly or Fry (11 R) ★★
4 The Warren Route (10+) ★★
6 Streets of Fire (10+) ★★
8 B & M (10+) ★
3
4
4
6
8

10 **Wired Bliss (11+)** ★ Obvious flaring crack going over a short bulge. Gear: To #2 Friend. FA: Bob D'Antonio and Brent Kertzman, 1984.

11 **B.M. (13 or B2)** Short and hard seam just right of *Wired Bliss.* Gear: Small cams. FA: Bob Murray and Bob D'Antonio, 1984.

CAMP ROCK (8.5 MILES)

Another roadside crag right at the entrance to Spillway campground. Good place to start leading or to set up topropes.

1 **Unknown (10)** Up face past bolts to an overhang and the top. FA: Unknown.

2 **Cave Crack (6)** ★ Obvious wide crack on left side of the rock. Gear: To #3 Friend. FA: Unknown.

3 **Log Jam (7)** ★ Goes up the wide crack just right of *Cave Crack.* Gear: To #4 Friend. FA: Unknown.

BABOON ROCK (8.5 MILES)

This excellent peice of granite has some of the best routes in the canyon. The approach is short with easy access to camping and fine bouldering making it a must stop for visiting climbers. See topo on page 48.

1 **Cats on a Hot Tin Roof (11–)** ★ Starts just left of a big chimney on the left side of the rock. Gear: Rack to #3 Friend. FA: Jeff Rhoads and Mike Sullivan, 1986.

2 **Unfinished Business (11–)** ★ Joins *Cats....* after 40 feet. Gear: Rack to #3 Friend. FA: Kevin Patno, 1986.

3 **Fly or Fry (11 R)** ★★ A Gallagher classic! Somewhat runout, this route is still one of the best routes on the rock. Gear: RPs, Stoppers and various other camming gear. FA: Peter Gallagher and John Kato, 1980.

4 **The Warren Route (10+)** ★★ This route is pretty hard to miss. Gear: To #3.5 Friend. FA: Robert Warren and John Kato, 1980.

5 **Something's Burning (11)** ★★ Great crack climbing on excellent rock with good protection. Gear: To #3 Friend. FA: Jeff Rhoads and Mike Sullivan, 1986.

6 **Streets of Fire (10+)** ★★ Starts the same as *Something's Burning,* but goes right when the crack makes a "Y." Gear: To #3 Friend. FA: Jeff Rhoads and Mike Sullivan, 1986.

Just east of Baboon Rock lies the Corridor Crag. To approach the crag take the nature trail from the first campsite at Spillway Campground. No topos are provided for these routes.

7 **No Surrender (11+ R)** ★★ A good climb with hard to place gear. Gear: To #2.5 Friend. FA: Bob D'Antonio and Peter Gallagher, 1982.

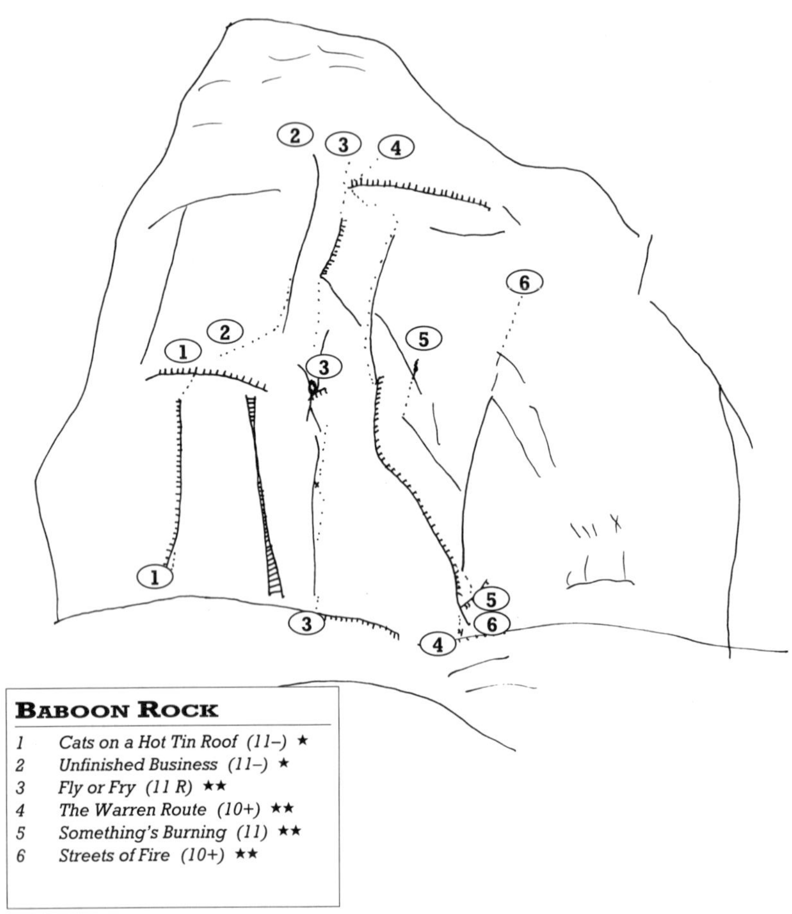

8 **B & M (10+) ★** Take the obvious crack out a short roof. Gear: To #3 Friend. FA: Bob D'Antonio and Mark Rolofson, 1983.

9 **Corridor Crack (10) ★★** Obvious thin crack inside the corridor. Gear: To #2.5 Friend. FA: Andy Brown and Lotus Steele, 1986.

10 **The Cosmic Crack (9) ★★** This crack is located on a block on the summit of Baboon Rock. Gear: To #2.5 Friend. FA: Mark Rolofson and Bob D'Antonio (Solo.).

ICICLE SLAB (8.7 MILES)

This is the obvious rock with a huge roof just west of Baboon Rock.

1 **Sublimation (10–) ★** Climb the center crack up the slab. Gear: Rack to #3 Friend. FA: Brian Blackstock and Rick Lince, 1986.

2 **Spuds Man (11–) ★** Follow the crack system just right of Sublimation. Gear: To #3 Friend. FA: Jeff Rhoads? 1986.

THE FORTRESS (8.9 MILES)

This extensive crag offers a number of high quality routes with great views overlooking Elevenmile Dam. The crag is broken into two tiers both accessed from the Spillway Campground.

1 **Shot on Sight (10+) ★** This route starts on the southwest face of the lower tier. Pitch 1 takes a low-angle crack to a belay ledge. Pitch 2 follows a crack out a short roof to low-angle slabs and a belay. Gear: To #3 Friend. FA: Jeff Rhoads and Mike Sullivan, 1986.

2 **The Barbwire Fence (9) ★** Starts on the ledge where *Shot on Sight* ends. Follow crack on left side of ledge. Gear: Rack to #3 Friend. FA: Jeff Rhoads and Mike Sullivan, 1986.

3 **The Electric Fence (11–) ★** Takes the crack on the right side of the ledge where *Shot on Sight* ends. Gear: Rack to #3 Friend. FA: Jeff Rhoads and Mike Sullivan, 1986.

4 **Thief of Rock (12) ★** Gear: #2 Friend. FA: Bob D'Antonio, 1985.

5 **The Hurting (12 R)** Don't fall, the gear is not the best. Gear: To #2 Friend. FA: Bob D'Antonio, 1985.

6 **Rock Busters (12) ★** Takes the dogleg crack down and right of *The Hurting*. Gear: To #3 Friend. FA: Richard Aschert and Bob D'Antonio, 1985.

7 **Canyon Classic (11+) ★** Very strenuous, keep moving on this one. Gear: To #3.5 Friend. FA: Neil Cannon, Bob D'Antonio, Richart Aschert and Dave Dangle, 1985.

8 **Let There Be Rock (12–) ★★** Good face climbing with excellent protection. Gear: Quickdraws. FA: Glen Schuler and Mark Milligan, 1991.

9 **Vapor Drawings (10+) ★★** Great climbing on good rock and position. Gear: Rack to #3 Friend. FA: Darrly Roth, Dave Dangle and Richard Aschert, 1986.

10 **Bits and Pieces (11+) ★★★** One of the best routes in the canyon, a must do. Gear: Rack to #2.5 Friend. FA: Richard Aschert, Bob D'Antonio and Dave Dangle, 1985.

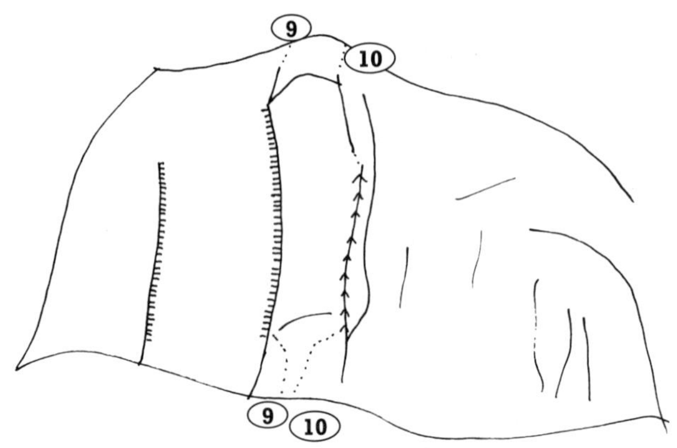

THE FORTRESS

1	*Shot on Sight (10+)* ★
2	*The Barbwire Fence (9)* ★
3	*The Electric Fence (11–)* ★
4	*Thief of Rock (12)* ★
5	*The Hurting (12 R)*
6	*Rock Busters (12)* ★
7	*Canyon Classic (11+)* ★
8	*Let There Be Rock (12–)* ★★
9	*Vapor Drawings (10+)* ★★
10	*Bits and Pieces (11+)* ★★★

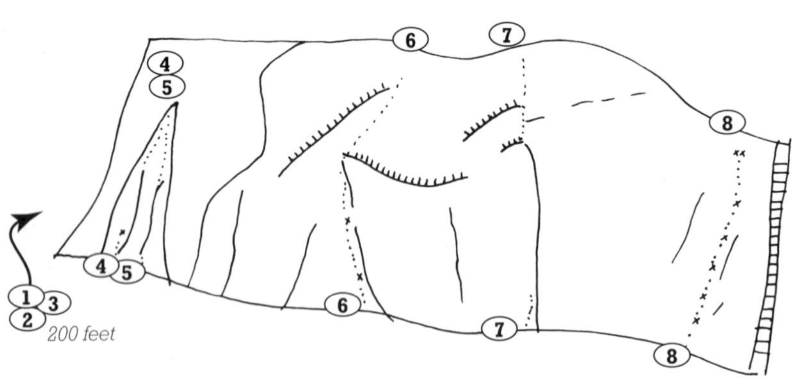

THE FORTRESS

6	*Rock Busters (12)* ★
7	*Canyon Classic (11+)* ★
9	*Vapor Drawings (10+)* ★★
10	*Bits and Pieces (11+)* ★★★

Yellow Thang (5.11b), Four Mile Dome. Photo by Stewart M. Green.

INDEX

Bolded numbers refer to topos or photos of the feature or route. Formations and areas are in all captials.

M

N

O

P

R

S

Access: It's everybody's concern

the ACCESS FUND

The Access Fund, a national, non-profit climbers' organization, is working to keep you climbing. The Access Fund helps preserve access and protect the environment by providing funds for land acquisitions and climber support facilities, financing scientific studies, publishing educational materials promoting low-impact climbing, and providing start-up money, legal counsel and other resources to local climbers' coalitions.

Climbers can help preserve access by being responsible users of climbing areas. Here are some practical ways to support climbing:

- **Commit yourself to "leaving no trace."** Pick up litter around campgrounds and the crags. Let your actions inspire others.
- **Dispose of human waste properly.** Use toilets whenever possible. If none are available, choose a spot at least 50 meters from any water source. Dig a hole 6 inches (15 cm) deep, and bury your waste in it. *Always pack out toilet paper* in a Ziploc™-type bag.
- **Utilize existing trails.** Avoid cutting switchbacks and trampling vegetation.
- **Use discretion when placing bolts and other "fixed" protection.** Camouflage all anchors with rock-colored paint. Use chains for rappel stations, or leave rock-colored webbing.
- **Respect restrictions that protect natural resources and cultural artifacts.** Appropriate restrictions can include prohibition of climbing around Indian rock art, pioneer inscriptions, and on certain formations during raptor nesting season. Power drills are illegal in wilderness areas. *Never chisel or sculpt holds in rock on public lands, unless it is expressly allowed* – no other practice so seriously threatens our sport.
- **Park in designated areas,** not in undeveloped, vegetated areas. Carpool to the crags!
- **Maintain a low profile.** Other people have the same right to undisturbed enjoyment of natural areas as do you.
- **Respect private property.** Don't trespass in order to climb.
- **Join or form a group to deal with access issues in your area.** Consider clean-ups, trail building or maintenance, or other "goodwill" projects.
- **Join the Access Fund.** To become a member, *simply make a donation (tax-deductible) of any amount.* Only by working together can we preserve the diverse American climbing experience.

The Access Fund. Preserving America's diverse climbing resources.

The Access Fund • P.O. Box 17010 • Boulder, CO 80308